Lost Restaurants
OF
GRAND RAPIDS

NORMA LEWIS

AMERICAN PALATE

Published by American Palate
A Division of The History Press
Charleston, SC
www.historypress.net

Copyright © 2015 by Norma Lewis
All rights reserved

Front cover: Upper right image of the exterior of the Schnitzelbank Restaurant
courtesy of the Grand Rapids Public Library.

First published 2015

Manufactured in the United States

ISBN 978.1.46711.887.3

Library of Congress Control Number: 2015953066

This one is for friends, especially Christine Nyholm, and in memory of Linda Butcher and Rosalie Moore.

Contents

Acknowledgements

A huge thank-you to the always knowledgeable and ever helpful staff at the Grand Rapids Public Library Local History Department. Especially Tim Gleisner, head of special collections, for his help in finding hidden treasure, and Julie Tabberer for the great job she did on many of the scans in this book. Thanks also to Alex Forist, collection curator at the Grand Rapids Public Museum. Elaine Snyder from the Byron Museum and Historical Museum and Elizabeth Druga, audiovisual archivist at the Gerald R. Ford Presidential Library, provided images. Thank you. Also, kudos to the unknown and unsung people everywhere who save old photographs and old stories that make local histories possible to re-create.

I am indebted to Jeff Lobdell, president of Restaurant Partners Inc., who generously shared his intimate knowledge of the Grand Rapids restaurant scene. And to Tom Maas from the Wyoming Historical Commission for not only his help but also his enthusiasm for this project. Thanks, too, to Rick Mack at the Choo Choo, Matt Dowdy, Bill Koski and Matt Rule at the Gilmore Collection, as well as Dan Verhill at the Cottage Bar.

A huge thank-you to Krista Slavicek, who held my hand when necessary and gently guided me through the History Press process, and Ryan Finn for a terrific edit. Any errors are mine alone. Thanks also to all the behind-the-scenes people at Arcadia Publishing/The History Press who work so hard making great things happen.

I appreciate the help and support given by my friends at the West Michigan Writer's Workshop. You're the best! My granddaughter Shelby Ayers stepped up when I needed her, and so did my daughter, Rhonda Ayers. I love you both and thank you.

Introduction

Nothing evokes more memories than food—what we ate, where we ate it and with whom. Grand Rapids has a rich history of restaurants serving up meals and precious memories since its earliest days. Some have been gone too long to be remembered by anyone today, but they left an indelible mark on the fledgling city on the rapids. Early settlers started them out of necessity.

In more recent times, others have come and gone, some opened by colorful entrepreneurs and patronized by even more colorful residents and visitors. Many became so popular that they are still missed and have become an important part of our local lore.

We remember the tastes, aromas and atmosphere of those gone but not forgotten venues that shaped our lives. We will never forget where we went on a first date with a future spouse or, conversely, the scene of our most cringe-worthy date. The places we celebrated graduations, engagements, anniversaries, retirements and birthdays. Also, those everyday favorites, including lunch counters, diners and malt shops where, like the television *Cheers* bar, everybody knew your name. Spots that had a real sense of place, unlike today's offerings, where, if you are traveling, it's impossible to tell whether you are scarfing down your burger and fries in Hartford, Houston or Hong Kong.

CHAPTER 1

In the Beginning

$\mathcal{A}$s in most fledgling cities, the majority of the earliest restaurants were found in hotels. The average family ate out only on special occasions, and singles often lived in boardinghouses, where their meals were furnished. Immigrants trying to put down roots in their new city usually didn't have disposable income for dining out. The Dutch, in particular, were known for their frugality. But those who mocked them at the time were later impressed when that tight-fistedness soon made it possible for them to buy homes and start businesses. Over time, they became the city's leading philanthropists.

Newcomers find the downtown streets confusing, if not annoying. Looking for a highly touted restaurant can be a challenge. They soon learn that the city was laid out in a peculiar pattern due to the preferences—or, as some would say, pigheadedness—of rival settlers Lucius Lyon and Louis Campau. Lyon was a surveyor, among his many talents, and his contribution resulted in a neatly ordered grid.

Campau, a fur trader, chose a crazy-quilt maze of old Indian trails blazed by the Ottawa Indians, the second group of Native Americans to settle here. The first were the Hopewells. One path is said to be a cow trail. In his entertaining book, *The Yesterdays of Grand Rapids*, Charles Belknap stated that Grandville Avenue was actually a trail made by a homesick cow who became lost in the woods and took a convoluted route back to the barn. Belknap arrived on the scene at age eight.

The two men also disagreed on what to call the growing area. Campau named the seventy-two acres he had bought for ninety dollars in 1826

Grand Rapids, while Lyon chose Kent as the name of his holdings north of Campau's land. Grand Rapids won, and the area became a city in 1850. Actually, they both won, as the city of Grand Rapids is in Kent County.

John Ball, a prosperous lawyer for whom the John Ball Park and Zoo is named, relocated permanently to Grand Rapids in the spring of 1837. He wrote in *Images of the Grand River Valley* in the 1830s that "Uncle Louis Campau's mansion was still part of the Rathbun House." During his first visit to the city, Ball stayed and dined at the Eagle Hotel, the only available option.

In the mid-1800s, the area known as Grab Corners dominated the city. The unflattering nickname came from the abundance of poker rooms and sleazy bars, and it was later called Campau Square. It is located between Monroe Avenue and Canal Street, just before the infamous Highway 131 "S" curve.

Pioneers not lucky enough to have brought wives to cook for them either lived in boardinghouses or frequented the early cafés, taverns and hotel dining rooms. Among the Grab Corners options were, according to Belknap, a half dozen dives and several basement bars where men drank whiskey from tin cups. Saloon owners often served free lunches comprising delicacies that included sour beef, ham and salt-cured fish, all of which were spiced with horseradish and other condiments calculated to enhance the diner's thirst. The beer and alcohol flowed and more than made up for the free food.

Hotels included the Rathbun, the Eagle and the National. Belknap remembered living for three years close to the Rathbun and the mouthwatering aromas emanating from the hotel kitchen. The Eagle not so much, as that hotel's pork, cabbage and corned beef was the same fare he ate at home. The National was noted for an exceptionally delicious chicken pot pie.

The Rathbun House was located at Monroe Avenue and Waterloo Street, a convenient location for the businesses on Waterloo. The street was later renamed Market. On December 29, 1846, the hotel hosted a New Year's ball. Among the luminaries attending were Louis Campeau, John Ball and a virtual who's who of the furniture industry elite. A few years later, in 1861, a supper was held there preceding a Grand Military Ball at Luce's Hall. A notation stated that carriages would be in attendance at 7:00 p.m.

In 1878, the *Grand Rapids Times* reported that to fully understand the popularity of the Rathbun, one need only to visit the dining hall any noon or evening, when it was always filled to capacity with hundreds of strangers' faces greeting one another at every meal. It further explained that proprietors A.R. Antisdel and Charles Cumings insisted that "no spirituous liquors of any kind be served or kept in stock at the bar." This was attributed to the "high moral tone and true respectability of their well-kept establishment." Maybe that explains why so many resorted to lifting those tin cups at the Grab Corners bars.

A dinner bell summoned diners to the Rathbun. An African American man named George (last name unknown) was the official bell ringer. At that time, the population was nearly all white, so according to the local rumor mill, George had escaped from the South via the Underground Railroad. George put on a nightly show while announcing the specialties of the house. He would hit the gong and yell, "Roast beef!" or "Chicken!" followed by another gong or two and "Taters and gravy!" In between the gongs, he danced a few steps, but he saved his fanciest moves for announcing dessert. Children and even some adults gathered to watch the local version of a minstrel show.

It would be wonderful to know the stories buried deep within the brick and mortar of restaurant walls. A search of the Grand Rapids Public Library ephemera collection yielded a yellowed menu from the Clarendon Hotel. On Thanksgiving Day, November 28, 1901, proprietor H.W. Melenbacher offered starters of "Blue Points, Caviar on Toast, Bisque of Oysters, Pickled Peaches and Dressed Lettuce." Entrées consisted of "Baked Red Snapper with Gardener Sauce and Saratoga Chips, Boiled Capon with Salt Pork and Parsley Sauce, Salmi of Duck with Sweet Potatoes, Escalloped Lobster à la Delmonico, Prime Roast of Beef au jus and Young Roast Turkey with Chestnut Dressing and Cranberry Sauce."

A diner who wanted more on that day could order salmon salad, crushed potatoes, steamed potatoes, fried parsnips, early June peas or sugar corn. A sweet tooth could be sated with English plum pudding and brandy sauce, pumpkin pie, mince pie, champagne jelly, strawberry ice cream, assorted cake or fruit. Halfway down the menu, bold capital letters screamed, "Rum Punch." For sure no one went home hungry.

But what made the menu noteworthy was that someone had scrawled in the corner, "My Papa's first dinner he got alone." One could spin a whole story from that one short sentence. Who was Papa? Why was he eating alone on Thanksgiving Day, and why for the first time? And on what did he dine when faced with such a multitude of choices?

Four hotels have occupied the northwest corner of Monroe Avenue and Ionia Street. First was the Hinsdell House, built in 1835 by Myron Hinsdell. About four years later, Hinsdell sold the property to Canton Smith, who renamed it the National Hotel, previously mentioned for its signature chicken pot pie. It was destroyed by fire in 1872 and rebuilt as the Morton House. Among its distinguished visitors was President William McKinley.

Another famous Morton House guest went almost unnoticed. Indiana poet James Whitcomb Riley arrived after an exhausting day of travel and poetry readings in the Kalamazoo area. He registered as J.R. Riley and then retreated to his room for two days of rest and catching up on his correspondence. He eschewed the grand dining room, opting instead for room service. A few guests recognized him but respected his privacy and told no one until after he had checked out.

The Morton owners lured A.V. Pantlind from Chicago to run the enterprise, including the food service. He was known as the "Hotel King," and he brought with him his nephew, J. Boyd Pantlind, to serve as his assistant. A.V. held the position from 1874 until his death in 1896. At that time, J. Boyd was named to take his uncle's place as manager.

An elaborate after-church luncheon was served on Easter Sunday 1891. J. Boyd Pantlind, to whom no detail was ever too small, had menus printed that were harp-shaped and held together with a bow on the left side. The front cover depicted a beautifully painted harp. Entrées included broiled California salmon with duchess potatoes, boiled chicken with oyster sauce, prime rib, stuffed turkey and spring lamb. Following the menu's food choices were the words and music to five Easter carols. Two Bible verses filled the last page. We can assume that the diners enjoyed a lively singalong while musicians played music appropriate to the holiday. J. Boyd Pantlind left the Morton House in 1902.

Five years before his departure, J. Boyd Pantlind had installed a new elevator and celebrated the occasion by holding a day of businessman excursions. It's hard to imagine a time when the promise of riding in an elevator would lure busy men from their offices, but J. Boyd made it work. The event gave guests a round-trip elevator ride to the rooftop, where they were treated to lunch. In so doing, management was able to show off the new purchase and, at the same time, introduce the delights of the food service operations to those who had not already had the pleasure of tasting the wide variety of Morton House delicacies.

A menu from January 1, 1912, shows that guests were offered various soups, salads and desserts, along with punch. Entrée choices included baked red snapper, boiled leg of mutton, filet mignon, roast prime beef and roast chicken. It was noted that the water came from the spring on J. Boyd's farm. For the benefit of out-of-town hotel guests, the menu also listed nearby

This harp-shaped menu was specially produced for an Easter dinner in 1891 at the Morton House. Inside were the words and music to popular Easter carols and two Bible verses. *Grand Rapids Public Library. Right*: Back cover details of the menu. *Grand Rapids Public Library.*

entertainment. At the Powers Theater, May Robson appeared in *A Night Out*, while Norman Hackett appeared in *Satan Sanderson* at the Majestic. The Temple and the Orpheum both had vaudeville shows, and the Garrick featured *The Devil's Web*. Those seeking a more active outing were invited to roller skate at the Coliseum.

In December 1923, a rebuilt Morton House celebrated its grand reopening. A corporation comprising Grand Rapids furniture men spent $1.5 million on the new structure, and it was described as one of the finest in the country. Next to the main lobby, reached through the main entrance on Monroe Avenue, was the Palm Court and a women's lounge. Adjoining that was the main dining room, also reachable through a separate lobby entrance. That dining room could seat up to 150 people and was considered by many to be the loveliest room in the hotel. Décor included a coffered ceiling, side walls of walnut and ivory palm plaster. Furnishings, of course, were from the local factories, and old gold, green and cream made up the room's color scheme.

Since its earliest days, the Morton House was home to some of the city's most popular eateries. *Grand Rapids Public Library.*

The Ionia Avenue entrance opened into the elevator lobby and the door to the Fountain Room, where snacks and light lunches were served. The décor in that room evoked Pompeii with colorful walls and ceiling, black-and-red woodwork and black-and-white lighting fixtures. That sounds like a fancy spot to have a slice of lemon pie or a grilled cheese sandwich.

An advertisement from 1923 stated that the Morton House affords a standard of luncheon and dinner service particularly appealing to the business and professional fraternity. The table d'hôte luncheon in the English Grill room went for $0.75. The table d'hôte dinner in the same room was $1.00, and the most expensive dinner in the Italian Room cost $1.50. By then, W.C. Keeley was the managing director, and the facility could be booked for banquets and social activities. The Morton House entrance also led to the White and White soda fountain, known for its refreshing ice cream confections.

For a time, professor J.B. Leonard—fortuneteller, mind reader and psychic—plied his trade in the hotel and enjoyed popularity with the lunch crowd. Although disdained by some, Mayor E.B. Fisher was a believer and said, "The man told me things that no one knew except God and myself, and he performed miracles of the sort that would have condemned him to death a few years ago."

By 1950, the Morton House boasted three restaurant choices. The Morton House VDM ("Very Dry Martini") was the wildly popular specialty of the Serpentine Bar. The other two choices were the Boar's Head Room and the Skyline Room. There were twenty-five options on the relish tray, the beef was prime and there were a number of seafood and poultry entrées for those wishing alternatives. By that time, a room went for six dollars a night. Every room had a radio, and two hundred rooms boasted television sets. The Morton House and Sweet's Hotel were both designed by Chicago architects Holabird and Roche, the firm that designed Chicago's fabled Palmer House Hotel.

According to Z.Z. Lydens, who edited *A Look at Early Grand Rapids*, in 1887 "the city licensed 140 saloons, one for each 450 men, women, and child, which was a foolish ratio. Grand Rapids was the town to come to for a big city feeling, and people came from a wide radius, and included strangers on business from afar. The number of saloons was a barometer of the city's growing activity and importance, more than an indication of its morals."

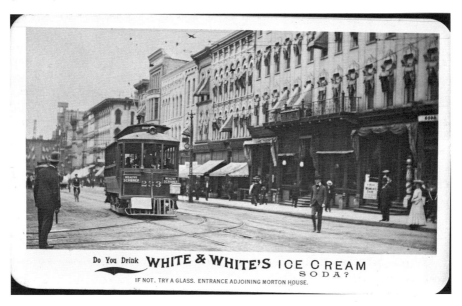

White and White had a soda fountain known far and wide for its refreshing ice cream confections. *Author's collection.*

In addition to more formal dining rooms, most hotels had a cafeteria. This one was in the Cody Hotel. *Grand Rapids Public Library.*

Another historic city hotel, the Cody, began in 1887 as a four-story structure called the Warwick and was built by Darwin D. Cody. Six years later, the Cody family added five more stories and took over running the establishment. The lobby and hotel offices had been on the second floor, with the first floor leased to retailers. As part of the change, the hotel reclaimed the entire first floor, adding a new lobby, a bar and a restaurant space.

At that time, they changed the name to the Cody Hotel. It benefited greatly from its prime downtown location at the southwest corner of Fulton Street and Division Avenue, the intersection that divides the city into quadrants. "Buffalo Bill" Cody was a cousin and often stayed in the hotel. Décor in the new lobby featured massive buffalo heads that had been given by Cousin Bill, who by all accounts was responsible for an ever-growing herd of headless buffalo. The dining rooms served hotel guests and invited the public in to dine as well. Fascination with the wild and woolly West was at an all-time high, so it's likely that those dining rooms were filled to capacity every time the legendary sharpshooter and showman visited his Michigan relatives.

The year 1935 brought a new cocktail lounge to the Cody. A *Grand Rapids Herald* headline called it the city's "Newest and Brightest Spot." The article described it as being as modern as tomorrow yet still carrying on the traditions of one of Grand Rapids' oldest institutions. During Prohibition, which began in Michigan on May 1, 1918, almost two years ahead of the rest of the country, the hotel's former bar had been turned into a pool hall, with a separate entrance on Fulton Street. By 1935, the alcohol ban had already been lifted for two years, and the Cody was ready to party. Toward that end, it claimed the largest liquor selection in town. The Cody was demolished in 1957 to make way for the City Municipal Parking Ramp No. 2. One more city landmark struck down in the name of the American obsession with cars.

Another of the early downtown hotels was the Rowe, the fourth one to occupy the northwest corner of Monroe Avenue and Michigan Street, following the Raasch, the Clarendon and the Charlevoix. Fred Rowe, who also owned the Valley City Milling Company, decided that Grand Rapids needed a new hotel and began construction. The new Rowe Hotel opened to great excitement in 1923, and it did not disappoint.

The Cody Hamburg Shop shortly before the hotel was razed. *Grand Rapids Public Library.*

Many of these sites go back to the days when Grand Rapids was walkable and people explored the city on foot. Later, when highways crisscrossed over the city, many drivers opted to get off at the exit closest to their destination, conduct their business and go back to the burbs. The ever-increasing cost of downtown parking made suburban eateries a better bargain. That has gradually changed as more and more condos are going up in the downtown area, both new construction and the conversion of some of the former furniture factories. Those new city dwellers needed more in the way of eateries and shopping. The big-name stores are all still in suburbia, but charming boutiques are opening amid the new restaurants and coffeehouses.

One newspaper ad for the new Rowe grandly proclaimed, "The Rowe Hotel invites you to Grand Rapids, the Gateway to the Playground of the Nation." "Playground of the Nation" sounds a bit over the top, but Grand Rapids is on the way to northern Michigan and the Upper Peninsula, popular tourist destinations for both summer and winter sports. The ad touted the English Room—with its rich tapestries, leaded glass and colorful paintings—as a backdrop for parties serving from 20 to 150 guests. Local residents were also urged to partake of the excellent cuisine in the dining room.

The Rowe Hotel honored the large Dutch immigrant population with this décor in its popular Dutch Room. *Grand Rapids Public Library.*

Lilly and Brea's Cafeteria as it appeared in 1915. *Grand Rapids Public Library.*

The Rowe's Dutch Room paid homage to the area's Dutch, at one time representing the largest immigrant group and still a major factor at 17 percent. A plate rail displayed blue-and-white Delft china and figurines of children in full Dutch dress. On one wall was a mural of a Netherlands village, complete with windmills. This appealed to visitors more than the local Dutch, many of whom still had their own wooden shoes at home.

Time did not treat the Rowe kindly, and in 1963, the building was sold to the American Baptist Home and Development Corporation and became an apartment building for seniors. The new owners changed the name to Olds Manor because of the large investment made by the heirs of automotive giant Ransom E. Olds. In 2001, Olds Manor closed its doors due to continuous financial losses, and the building remained vacant until it seemed certain that its future included a wrecking ball.

It received a last-minute reprieve when it was discovered that the building, despite outward appearances, was structurally sound. CWD Development partners Sam Cummins, Scott Weirda and Dan DeVos bought the property, and it is expected to reopen in the summer of 2016 with ten floors of renovated apartments and condominiums. The 9,500-square-foot first

Otto Sauerberg served fast food from Otto's Hamburg Wagon. He later upgraded and renamed it Ye Olde Wayside Grill in downtown Grand Rapids for four decades. *Photo circa 1930s. Grand Rapids Public Museum.*

floor will be used for restaurant and retail space. No word yet on what the restaurants will be. The property is also reverting back to its original name and will again be called the Rowe.

Cafeterias were favored by many, and of the local choices, some like the Cody and Niagara were in hotels. The Lilly and Brea occupied a free-standing building. Those casual dining options served a purpose in that they were both quick and inexpensive.

Otto Sauerberg performed a real service when he opened his early version of fast food, the primitive Otto's Hamburg Wagon stand on Monroe Avenue. It had grab-and-go appeal for anyone looking for a quick sandwich without bothering to go inside a café. He did so well that he had a shell placed over it to resemble a diner. The spruced-up eatery deserved a more impressive name, so Otto called it Ye Wayside Grille. He served street food for forty years beginning in 1906.

CHAPTER 2

Bentham's Restaurant, Sweet's Hotel, the Pantlind Hotel and the Amway Grand Plaza

One downtown block, Monroe Avenue between Pearl and Lyon Streets, has been the location of Grand Rapids' most renowned hotels and restaurants since the pioneer days.

It all started with a single restaurant, Bentham's, on the site where the elegant hotels would one day stand. From the 1830s through the 1850s, Bentham's dished up smoked venison, boiled ham and a rich venison stew simmered with onions. A kettle of pea soup drew in the French fur traders. Potential patrons lacking the funds to buy a meal could barter a muskrat pelt or other fur. Molasses candy was a favorite with all who tasted it and could be had for only a penny. The Cosmopolitan Restaurant and Bakery was also on that block for a short time.

Bentham's closed its doors in the late 1850s, and the spot became a sawmill pond until 1868. That's when Martin Sweet saw the potential for a hotel to serve traffic brought in by the growing furniture industry. He drained the pond and enlarged the Exchange Bank to make way for Sweet's Hotel, the crown jewel of Campau Square. Sweet was a prominent local businessman and served one term as mayor.

SWEET'S HOTEL

N.C. Johnson was the proprietor of the first Sweet's dining rooms and offered different menus according to the day of the week. On Sunday, August 31,

1884, the Five O'Clock Dinner menu listed chicken with corn or consommé for the soup course. Next, diners could choose from among three roasts, fricassée of spring chicken, breaded veal cutlets, pork and beans, whitefish, corned beef and cabbage, tongue or sugar-cured ham. Also on hand were seven cold dishes, including lobster; various relishes; and ten vegetables. Those still able to eat dessert found pastries, pies, cakes, fruits, puddings, ice cream and a light meringue pastry with the provocative name of French Kisses. Wine was available, along with tea (English or Japanese) and coffee. It can probably be assumed that anyone trying to shed a few pounds stayed away from Sweet's.

Another popular Sweet's Hotel restaurant was the Oyster Bay, located in the basement. It was noted in the *Grand Rapids Democrat* on November 26, 1874, that if a gentleman needed an added enticement to frequent Sweet's dining room, there was an abundance of ladies. The paper noted that on the previous day the tables were graced with "fully 150 of the other sex who were busy doing justice to a bill of fare of ample portions, and were regular boarders from some of the best families who had taken up their abode for

Sweet's Hotel as it looked when Tillie the Terrible Swede stayed there when she came to town to demonstrate her bicycle-racing style. *Author's collection.*

The Niagara Cafeteria was located in Sweet's Hotel. *Grand Rapids Public Library.*

the winter. All travelers are fortunate in having a place of sojourn where the presence of so many of the fair sex is found. Their society always adds a charm to any hotel, and Sweet's is indeed fortunate in having so many of the charmers."

The following year, the hotel made some changes, including the installation of the only hotel elevator in the city. The *Grand Rapids Democrat* noted that "the table is even better than formerly, and no expense is spared to have the freshest and best of all the market affords." All that grandeur and girls, too.

Tillie the Terrible Swede stayed at Sweet's in the late 1890s during her reign as the top women's bicycle racer in the world. Originally from Sweden, Tillie Anderson immigrated to Chicago at age fourteen. It's unclear why Tillie was considered "Terrible." Perhaps because women who participated in competitive sports were frowned upon. More likely it was because the riding costumes she designed and made consisted of form-fitting pants and tops. The pants clearly showed her leg muscles, prompting one reporter to comment that God never intended for women to resemble horses. In Tillie's defense, speed riding in the cumbersome skirts of the day would have been suicidal. Bicycle racing was the most popular spectator sport during that short window of time around the turn of the twentieth century, and Tillie gave a well-attended demonstration on Ionia Street. Even those finding her uniform offensive could not help being impressed with her athletic ability. It's said she kept the dining room staff hopping providing her with her training regimen of salmon, sardines and oysters.

The Knickerbocker Society of Grand Rapids held its second annual banquet at Sweet's on February 7, 1901. Membership comprised the upper crust of the local Dutch community, and every item on the special menu was underscored with a bit of poetry. Under celery, "a brittle glory"; sweet potatoes, "let the sky rain with potatoes"; shrimp salad, "a dish fit for the gods"; and roast domestic duck, "till death untimely stopped my tuneful tongue." Queen Wilhelmina sat on the Netherlands throne at the time, so under the Wilhelmina Punch, the verse read, "Be to her virtues very kind; be to her faults a little blind." The line at the bottom of the page, of course, announced that "all is well that ends well."

By then, the hotel was struggling financially, and bookings like the Knickerbocker event became fewer. As grand as Sweet's Hotel was thought to be, the best was yet to come. When it came, it bore the name Pantlind. Like his uncle before him, J. Boyd Pantlind had a solid background in hotel and restaurant management. He decided that the time was ripe for him to have his own hotel.

Although Sweet's Hotel and restaurants have been gone for more than a century, it is still possible to lunch in Martin Sweet's Italianate mansion, now owned by the Women's City Club of Grand Rapids. Back when white-gloved, chapeau-wearing ladies lunched out on a regular basis, there were two local favorites: the Home Tea Room and the Women's City Club. The Home Tea Room, once located on Lafayette Street, is long gone. The Women's City Club still serves lunches on a reservation-only basis in its dining room, named Desdemona's in honor of Martin Sweet's wife. One can still get a small taste of the elegance enjoyed by Desdemona Sweet and other privileged ladies-who-lunched in days gone by. And one can enjoy it in the same house where Desdemona herself welcomed the who's who of Grand Rapids society to dine at her lavishly set table.

The building is at 254 Fulton Street in the Heritage Hill neighborhood. Heritage Hill is one of the country's largest urban historic districts, with about 1,300 houses that date from the mid-1800s. Although Desdemona's is in the Italianate-style building, the area boasts fifty-nine other architectural styles as well.

THE PANTLIND HOTEL

J. Boyd bought the Sweet's Hotel in 1902 and renamed it the Pantlind Hotel in honor of his beloved uncle, who had taught him how to excel in the hospitality business. It became an immediate favorite with those attending the semiannual furniture markets held in January and July.

He practiced micromanagement and oversaw every detail. Of the food service, he said, "Give them soup first, and they won't want so much meat. What you lose on food, you make up for on the liquor." More than a century later, restaurants still depend on alcohol consumption to inflate the bottom line.

There was one unanticipated problem. The Pantlind Hotel's restaurants and the numerous other eateries scattered around the city produced mountains of garbage. Early garbage collectors took their offerings to piggeries located just west of the downtown area. No doubt the stench of rotting garbage detracted from an otherwise pleasant downtown ambience, but it seems unlikely that the pigs were any less malodorous. J. Boyd considered himself a gentleman farmer as well as a hotel man, so he insisted on keeping hotel restaurant garbage for his own pigs. For a time, he prevailed, and his swine pigged out on the best garbage in town.

That stopped when Mayor George Ellis decided to challenge him. The mayor called dibs on the hotel's garbage, saying that it was city property and should be fed to city pigs, not those belonging to J. Boyd. He took Pantlind to court and won what may go down in history as the only custody case the court ever heard involving ownership of restaurant garbage.

Z.Z. Lydens shared this memory of that colorful time in Grand Rapids' past: "The history of the piggeries was erratic and at one point hilarious. In one day's garbage there was a large quantity of peaches pickled in alcohol. The pigs got drunk, squealing merrily, and staggering as their legs gave way, pitching them forward on their snouts." The author didn't disclose which restaurant was responsible for the snockered swine.

It wasn't long before enlightened sanitation practices brought the "Garbage Wars" to an end, and J. Boyd's pigs, along with the municipal porkers, were evicted from hog heaven.

Over the next years, Pantlind made improvements to his hotel but was still not quite satisfied. In 1913, he decided to rebuild completely. The new hotel was opened in December 1914 and was an instant sensation. It stood twelve stories tall, was fireproof and had not one but three elevators. It was billed as "the most beautifully furnished hotel in the United States,"

J. Boyd Pantlind's hotel took up an entire block and boasted 750 rooms. *Author's collection.*

which should have come as no surprise since it was located in Grand Rapids, then known as Furniture City. All the furnishings came from local manufacturers. Most of the 750 rooms came with private baths. Rooms without baths were $1.50 per night. A private bathroom drove the price up to $2.00 or more. The Pantlind was soon rated one of the top ten hotels in the country. Not bad for a city some still considered a backwater town in the wilds of southwest Michigan.

With the fancy new hotel came fancy new restaurants. The main dining room, also called the Grille, had a vaulted ceiling with the wood paneled in French gray. Imported French tiles covered the floor, and six chandeliers illuminated the space. Soft music played in the background.

On the mezzanine level were two writing rooms; the one for the ladies' use had silk upholstered chairs and settees, floor lamps, plants and fresh flowers. The desks were proportioned for women. The men's writing room had direct access to the bar and larger mahogany desks, with a lamp on each. It might have been assumed that ladies couldn't write and imbibe at the same time. More likely it was because men staying in the hotel were usually thought to be in town taking care of business and had important matters to work on. Women, it was likely assumed, were probably only dashing off wish-you-were-here postcards to those back home.

The Colonial Room, also called the Breakfast Room, was arguably one of the most beautifully decorated rooms in the hotel. Though square, a center dome gave it a circular appearance. The floor was carpeted and the walls paneled in ivory and rose tones. Light from crystal chandeliers and gold lamps on the tables around the perimeter gleamed on the perfectly polished mahogany chairs. Elaborate window treatments were the finishing touches. The décor was Adamesque, the eighteenth-century Neoclassical style attributed to Scottish brothers John, Robert and James Adam.

Although already known as the best in town, and one of the ten best in the country, Pantlind believed that his hotel could be even better. He beefed up his food service operations by hiring a new dining room manager. The announcement read: "Since the end of the 19th century, the name Pantlind has meant hospitality, delicious food, attentive service, and a genial atmosphere which have combined and increased steadily with the years. From the days of the old second floor dining room of the refurnished and renamed Sweet's Hotel, to the Magnificent Pantlind Hotel of today, with its many public and private dining rooms, quality foods prepared by expert chefs and served

The Colonial Room, also called the Breakfast Room, in the Pantlind Hotel in 1937. *Grand Rapids Public Library.*

in clean hospitable surroundings, [establishments] have added enjoyment to simple repasts and pompous functions for Grand Rapids residents and travelers from the world around."

He then went on to say that he had appointed Louis W. Blasy as dining room manager. Blasy's credentials showed that his most recent job had been manager of the Tip Top Inn in Chicago; during his twenty-seven years in the business, he had been associated with the finest hotels and restaurants of America and Europe. That pretty much guaranteed that hosting those "pompous functions" would continue to be an important part of the Pantlind food service operations for a long time to come.

Despite Blasy's rarified résumé, he ran the operation in a way that prices remained relatively affordable. For example, the Main Dining Room menu offered a typical dinner for $1.50 and listed choices of starters, side dishes and desserts. Entrée choices were a gourmet's dream come true, with stuffed lobster; grilled Blythefield Farm chicken (Blythefield Farm was on the site of the present-day Blythefield Country Club), roast larded filet of beef, sweetbreads and Virginia ham Eugenie or cold roast duckling with currant jelly. Breakfasts started at $0.55 and went all the way up to $1.00, while $1.00 also bought a table d'hôte luncheon. To put that in perspective, this took place during a time when a housewife could buy a week's groceries for $5.00 or less. Dining out was still a luxury, though a luxury worth the occasional indulgence.

It's easy to imagine those dining tables set with starched white tablecloths, polished silver, spotless crystal, gleaming china and fresh flower centerpieces. Add waiters giving impeccable service and soft background music and you have a perfect recipe for a total dining experience that made even the best food taste better still. What a perfect way for locals to enjoy life's most special moments or for out-of-towners to unwind after an exhausting day of business or travel. How pampered those long-ago diners must have felt.

Furniture markets brought in buyers from all over the country, and it was necessary to accommodate those visitors. It became equally necessary to promote the city as a convention destination so that all those new hotel rooms and dining spots would not be empty the rest of the year. With the exception of office furnishings and commercial seating, the furniture industry has long since departed the city, seduced by the financial incentives offered by North Carolina. Despite that loss, Grand Rapids still enjoys a brisk convention business.

By the 1920s, the local Rotary, Kiwanis, Lions, Optimist and Zonta Clubs all held weekly lunch meetings in one of the Pantlind restaurants.

Corporations found the meeting suites and ballrooms the perfect places to hold conferences, and company social events ranging from retirement celebrations to Christmas parties. They were always popular wedding reception venues.

Fred Z. Pantlind, son of J. Boyd and second-in-command, sang the praises of the hotel's Electric Grill with a notice:

> *The increasing popularity of Thursday evening dinner dances in the Electric Grill, makes it imperative to extend the program of dinner dances to include Saturday evenings also.*
>
> *These affairs have become a weekly event with many Grand Rapids residents and hotel guests who appreciate good music and a few dances, as well as the good food prepared in the incomparable Electric Grill. Drop in any Thursday or Saturday evening at the dinner hours 6 to 8 P.M.*

A postscript offered further enticement to come to dine at the hotel:

> *And if you haven't already enjoyed one of the National Dishes, including six nationalities, served by attendants in the costumes of those nations, in the CAFETERIA, don't let yourself miss this treat any longer than tomorrow.*

The Pantlind hired Frederick Rathaas as pastry chef in 1928. He came with vast experience in creating European-style desserts sure to delight sophisticated palettes, and he also introduced pie-topped-with-ice-cream-loving Americans to new treats from the other side of the ocean. Rathaas had previously worked in Germany, France and Switzerland and had apprenticed with the bakers who supplied the German Duke of Baden.

December 20, 1947, marked the opening of the Pantlind's Mocha Room, where patrons were invited for luncheon, dinner or supper dancing to the music of Jerry Shelton. The new spot also had a Mocha Terrace for cocktails.

The Pantlind always provided multiple dining options, from top-of-the-line elegance to the lowly coffee shop. A postcard, dating back to when it cost only a penny to mail, boasts 750 rooms and a whole city block of hospitality. Numerous restaurants have come and gone during the years between. VIPs who dined in those fabled halls include two prominent political figures from Grand Rapids: longtime U.S. senator Arthur Vandenberg and, more recently, Grand Rapids congressman turned president Gerald R. Ford. Ford was born in Nebraska but moved here at about a year old. His mother's second husband adopted him when he was three.

Patrons liked the Mocha Room because their entrées were carved to order. *Grand Rapids Public Library.*

Ramona Park and Bigelow Field, two more gone-but-not-forgotten Grand Rapids institutions, were the scene of numerous sports and entertainment events and drew the likes of Jimmy Durante, Jack Benny, Babe Ruth, Duke Ellington and thousands of other celebrities, nearly all of whom slept and dined at the Pantlind.

The top-floor penthouse was where locals enjoyed steak soup on Sunday afternoon and late suppers and drinks after attending the theater or simply stopped for a nightcap after a night on the town. Its ambience included views of the city lights. Lu Brady remembered stopping there one evening in 1976 with a date she was trying hard to impress. She did, but not in the way she had hoped. As they sat across from each other in a booth by a window, he asked her what was straight down. Of course, the only way to see straight down was to move closer to the window.

Not realizing that the seat cushion slid with her when she slid toward the window, and also not realizing that there was a gap between the end of the booth and the window, her end of the cushion went down the rabbit hole, while the opposite end shot straight up. For a moment, Lu was on the floor, wedged between the booth and the floor-to-ceiling window—and embarrassed in the extreme. Her embarrassment worsened when the young woman serving burst into a fit of uncontrollable giggles as she approached them. She had to walk away to compose herself three times before she was able to take their order. Even then, she giggled whenever she brought them something or had to pass them on her way to another table. When Lu visited the ladies' room, the woman was also there; once again, she lost it. "It was so much fun having you here tonight," she finally managed to blurt out.

If the bartender thought it was funny, he did a better job of hiding it and insisted that their drinks were on the house. The evening mercifully ended at Lu's front door, and although she tried apologizing again for the fiasco, her date quickly shushed her. "Let's go back next Saturday," he said. "Think you could do that again?" He had descended from one of those frugal Dutch immigrant families mentioned earlier and believed that a little public humiliation was a small price to pay if it resulted in free drinks.

The Pantlind Hotel's lower-level Knife and Fork Coffee Shop was best known for its luncheon plate–sized burgers. It stayed open 24/7, making it convenient for locals to drop in for a quick snack before heading home. Hotel guests could take the elevator down and avoid the high cost of room service. Other favorites during the Pantlind years included the casual Back Door Saloon, serving up drinks and sandwiches in a piano bar setting, and the Town Hall's beer and sandwiches were lunch favorites—but only if you didn't mind waiting for a table. The Cypress Cellar and the Charcoal Inn served multicourse dinners, and there was also a cafeteria. In all its incarnations, the hotel maintained several restaurants so as to appeal to the different needs of its clientele.

AMWAY GRAND PLAZA HOTEL

But nothing lasts forever. Just as Sweet's Hotel before it, the once elegant Pantlind grew shabby. Amway Corporation's co-founders and local philanthropists Rich DeVos and Jay Van Andel bought the fading beauty and restored it to its former glory. After extensive renovations, the new Amway Grand Plaza Hotel opened in 1981 and was once again a first-class hotel and home to first-class restaurants.

The new owners had seemingly done the impossible. They had wisely chosen restoration over gutting and starting over. So, while the hotel sparkled fresh and new, it retained its historic charm. The exterior appeared hardly changed at all, and the transformed lobby, though different, seemed familiar as well. Despite its makeover, the new look was compatible with the old, and the overall look once again exuded the refined elegance visitors had grown to expect. A "glass tower" addition on the back part of the building brought the hotel into modern times.

The restaurants following the renewal ran from the opulent white tablecloth establishments to the casual throw-your-peanut-shells-on-the-floor and everything in between. Tootsie Van Kelly's was an immediate favorite among hotel guests as well as locals out on the town. Dark wood and distressed leather were the muted décor of the Lumber Baron's Room, evocative of a British men's club harkening back to a time when "gentlemen's club" wasn't synonymous with strip joint. Picture instead the room in an old palatial estate where the men adjourned for cigars and an after-dinner brandy.

The ballroom has long been the scene of posh wedding parties, society bashes and a wide assortment of corporate shindigs. With impeccable service, great food and plenty of room for a band and dancing, it was, and continues to be, the first choice of such event planners.

Since the beginning, owners have been innovative and allowed in-house dining options to evolve with the ever-changing tastes of the fickle public. In 2011, Ruth's Chris Steak House moved into the coveted space on the northeast end of the first floor. Although it is a chain, it's a small one and is a nice fit with the hotel's practice of serving only the best. It has been well received, even though it replaced the 1913 Room, Michigan's only five-diamond restaurant and named for the year J. Boyd Pantlind rebuilt the Pantlind Hotel.

To the dismay of some, a Starbucks coffee shop took up residence in the southeast corner, thus marking the end of an era where manifestations of the city's unique character once prevailed.

The Amway Grand Plaza gave a nod to the past with a new restaurant named Bentham's, the name of the first restaurant on that Monroe Avenue site. The new Bentham's appropriated the name but bore no other similarity to its namesake. One major difference is that if someone came in with a muskrat pelt to trade for dinner, he would be politely but firmly shown the door. Bentham's closed in 2014 to make room for a Wolfgang Puck restaurant expected to open in the late fall of 2015, to be called the Kitchen Counter by Wolfgang Puck.

CHAPTER 3

Fine Dining

FISK LAKE TAVERN

On the banks of Fisk Lake, in what is now East Grand Rapids, was the Fisk Lake Tavern. A trail that became the present-day Robinson Road led east from the city through thick forests and over multiple streams to a lovely lake. John W. Fisk followed the trail and liked what he saw. In 1837, he built a log tavern overlooking the lake he had named Fisk Lake. Two years later, he sold the business to James Fosget, who was married to a former New Englander related to Presidents John and John Quincy Adams and described as being "as fine an example of American womanhood as the valley ever welcomed." Jerome Trowbridge was the next owner, followed by Napoleon B. Carpenter. Boney, as Carpenter was called, ran the tavern with his wife, "Auntie" Carpenter, who was a great cook and loved by all.

By the 1870s, the Fisk Lake Tavern had been completely rebuilt of fashionable brick, and the Carpenters had added a second story. It quickly become the favorite of the horsey crowd. Many Civil War veterans still had their horses and enjoyed both riding and racing them. Their ladies were excellent horsewomen despite the long, cumbersome skirts of the day that made it necessary to ride sidesaddle. A pleasant day of riding included a stop at the tavern to place their dinner orders, followed by galloping over the countryside to ride along the Thornapple River in what is now suburban Cascade. A scrumptious evening meal capped an idyllic day in the country.

Dining at the Fisk Lake Tavern was a perfect finale to a day of horseback riding or sleigh rides. *Grand Rapids Public Library.*

Boney Carpenter served roasted chicken and what many called the "finest steaks that ever came from a charcoal broiler." The new structure had a second-floor ballroom. Dancing made what had already been a perfect day even better. Although Boney's middle initial was "B," and may or may not have stood for Bonaparte, he earned his nickname by playing the bones for his guests' enjoyment; the hand-held percussion instrument was originally used in folk music and was so named because, though now made of wood or plastic, it was originally made of animal bones.

Ellen Moore described a typical pleasure-filled day at the Fisk Lake house in *Early Days in the Grand River Valley*:

> *After sleigh rides, the crowds returned to a dinner of chicken pie or frog legs, hot coffee, fried cakes, and pie. Later the young people held a dance in the upper hall.*
> *Two men fiddled and took turns calling for the square dances. No one ever thought of "two-stepping." The long sleigh ride with straw to cover the bottom and buffalo robes for warmth, the prancing horses and jingling bells, the giggling girls and shouting boys gave an added zest for the supper and the quadrilles. We did not reach home until the wee small hours.*

The building was razed in the early 1900s, leaving only precious memories of a simpler time.

Hattem's Restaurant

Deeb Hattem immigrated from Lebanon with his family, and his first business venture was in retail. He opened his restaurant in 1910 at 400 South Division, on the corner of Division and Wealthy, with his son, Moses, who eventually took over running the fine dining establishment. It was the kind of place where toasts were made, and if the toastmaster didn't have one at the ready, he could borrow from the examples printed on the multipage menu. Possibilities included "Here's to the man who loves his wife, and loves his wife alone, for many a man loves another man's wife when he ought to be loving his own" or "Here's to the wings of Love, May they never lose a feather. Here's that your shoes and my shoes will be under one bed together."

The menu also contained a few ads for the purveyors of products that the Hattems served, such as Michigan Bread, Kent Club Coffee and Sealtest Ice Cream. Ice cream concoctions were always popular and ranged from ten-cent sodas to the top-of-the-line banana splits and "fancy sundaes" listed at a quarter. One could get a martini for the same price as a hot fudge sundae.

The menu had a "Just for Fun" page with philosophical homilies like:

You will find, my dear boy, that the dearly prized kiss,
Which with rapture you snatched from the half-willing miss,
Is sweeter by far than the legalized kisses
You give the same girl when you've made her your Mrs.

Another notation stated that no sales under ten cents would be made in the cocktail room.

Hattem's was the kind of place a fella took his best girl for an evening of dining and dancing. Dinners started with cocktails and ended with Cuban cigars for the gentlemen. The dining experience was enhanced by nightly music on the Hammond organ. More often than not, that music was provided by Moses's wife, Maxine.

Maxine George had been a gifted musician living in Worcester, Massachusetts. She was also the child of Lebanese immigrants. By the time she was twelve years old, she was playing the organ between shows at area movie houses and had played with luminaries such as Spike Jones and accompanied the likes of Artie Shaw and Vic Damone. Artie Shaw invited her to join his group, but her parents still held their strict old-country values and wanted her to be home sleeping in her own bed every night.

The Hattem family—Moses behind the bar, as well as Maxine and Deeb—made certain that all who dined at Hattem's had an evening to remember. *Grand Rapids Public Library.*

In 1948, a church concert brought her to Grand Rapids, where she met Moses. They married two years later. Along with performing at the family restaurant, Maxine appeared at other venues in the area, including the Pantlind Hotel and Hudson's Department Store and at the weekly Lion's Club meetings. The busy lady also gave music lessons and recorded one album for RCA, *Music by Maxine.* The family belonged to the St. Nicholas Antochian Orthodox Church, where Maxine served as organist. She shared her music with residents of the Grand Rapids area for more than fifty years.

The Fords, Gerald and Betty, were Hattem's fans. Moses Hattem and Jerry Ford had been South High School classmates, and Betty, who had been a professional dancer, loved boogying to Maxine's beat. Ford's presidential calendar shows that on July 3, 1975, he met with the Hattems, their four children and Maxine's sister, Delores George, in the White House.

Hattem's Restaurant closed in 1968. As of the summer of 2015, its former location on the southeast corner of Division Avenue and Wealthy Street, across Wealthy from the Catholic Diocese complex, was a vacant lot. Moses

Hattem died in August 2005, and Maxine died eleven months later on July 17, 2006. Aquinas College established a scholarship in her name for music majors specializing in piano and organ playing.

The Schnitzelbank

The Schnitzelbank, a city icon for decades, first opened on Wealthy Street in 1934 and moved to Jefferson Avenue four years later. The décor, both interior and exterior, conjured up visions of the Black Forest and made one want to grab a stein and hum the "Drinking Song" from *The Student Prince. Prosit*!

It was owned by the Siebert family and managed by Karl Gustav Siebert for forty years. The inside imagery was painted by Wilhelm Seeger, an uncle of the owners. Anti-German sentiment that raged during the Nazi years threatened but never did lasting harm to the popular restaurant. American Germans didn't like the Nazis any more than other Americans did, so it was a moot point. Also, the food was just too good to boycott. Where else could you get weinerschnitzel that melts in your mouth, sip imported German beer and enjoy it in a setting that felt like Germany?

The Schnitzelbank served its food in an authentic German atmosphere. *Grand Rapids Public Library.*

The restaurant always had a loyal customer base, and employees were loyal as well. One waitress in particular, Beverly Byram, retired at age seventy-five after having worked there more than thirty-five years. The success enjoyed by the "Schnitz," as it was affectionately known, is probably what led to a number of other similarly named eateries, including the Swiss Chalet, Matterhorn, Rathskeller, Der Steak House, Bierstube and Bavarian Haus. All were popular in the middle of the twentieth century, although none remains today. While they were good, not one measured up to the Schnitz. Some were inspired only by the name and actually served good old American steak, but the Bierstube and Bavarian Haus served German food. It just wasn't as good as at the Schnitz.

The much-loved and greatly missed dining spot was sacrificed in 2008 to accommodate the need of additional parking space for the Mary Free Bed Rehabilitation Hospital.

SCOTTIES RESTAURANT AND LOUNGE

In 1952, Stan and Ann Kowalski opened a new Scotties restaurant on Division Avenue at Hall Street after the old one was destroyed by fire. The Kowalskis still served the same fine food and maintained the high level of service on which they had built a solid reputation. As Ann put it, "It seems to us that if the pleasure of good eating and drinking were removed entirely from the eternal scheme of things, this would be a sad world indeed."

They always did their best to make sure they were never the cause of that sad world and never compromised the eatery's reputation by skimping on the food and drink served in their establishment. Entrées included steaks, chops, seafood, barbecued ribs and live lobster.

The new site boasted a sparkling new cocktail bar, the Trade Winds Dining Room, and hosted banquets and other large group events in either the Trader or Hurricane Rooms. As the names suggest, a South Seas atmosphere—Balinese to be exact—lived up to its promise of delighting patrons from the former location, while also attracting new ones.

SAYFEE'S AND SAYFEE'S EAST

Kezma (Kez) Sayfee was a young man seeking adventure when he left Grand Rapids for the adventure of working on the Alcan Highway in

Alaska in 1943. Unfortunately for him, but fortunately for Grand Rapids, Sayfee flunked the physical. He returned home disappointed and with no inkling of what he wanted to do next. The decision was made when someone gave him money to run a bar on Division Avenue. He introduced Lebanese-style food to patrons, and his career was set.

His mother helped in the kitchen, turning out Kibbe, Yabrah and meat pies, items that remained on the menu, along with the steaks and seafood that American diners associated with fine dining. The restaurant reigned as a downtown institution until Kez Sayfee closed it and opened Sayfee's East, a stand-alone eatery near what was then called Eastbrook Mall at Twenty-eighth Street and East Beltline.

It soon became the go-to spot for dining and dancing in a sophisticated atmosphere without heavy metal, revolving lights or disco balls. The kind of place where those who preferred their dance music not played at deafening decibels have cherished memories of enjoying an exceptional dinner. They spent the rest of the evening enjoying a drink or two and doing the swing or dancing cheek to cheek. The restaurant closed in February 2011, leaving a hole that has yet to be filled.

Kez Sayfee's restaurants succeeded because of his commitment to giving his customers the best of food and service. Restaurants are among the first to suffer during bad economic times, but Sayfee refused to compromise and never cut corners on the products he served. Dinners out might be a less frequent splurge during recessions, but Kez believed that was all the more reason to make them memorable. Newly hired servers were given manuals that defined the company's requirements, along with useful tips such as "Help in any way you can to get your customer comfortable, relaxed, and make him feel at home." It also gave them something to think about with "If you don't care about service, why should they care about leaving you a tip?" That still resonates. Everyone can recall a few incidents where, had the servers been given that tip, they would have been happier with the tips given them.

FINGER'S GAY '90s

The Finger's Gay '90s Restaurant and Lounge on Northland Drive was known for its signature golden-crusted fried chicken. It was served with real mashed potatoes at a time when too many eateries had discovered the kind that came out of a box. Southern-style biscuits and gravy were served upon

Many still mourn the loss of Finger's fried chicken and the dazzling restrooms. *Author's collection.*

request. The restaurant was founded by Paul and Helen Finger in 1946 and stayed in business for more than fifty years. The owners were hands on and formed lifelong friendships with staff and customers alike.

Fried chicken wasn't the only thing for which Finger's was famous. It also had the only restroom in town with a fountain that was activated by the flush of the toilets.

Paul and Helen gave their establishment a theme before themes were expected, and theirs was theater. As the menu explained, "Around the turn of the century when a gentleman and his lady went out for an evening of pleasure, it often included a visit to the theater followed by a sumptuous dinner served amid the most elegant of surroundings. Among the most famous of the Broadway restaurants in New York City was Delmonico's while at the other end of the country the Carriage Trade frequented gracious restaurants of that era in the Nob Hill section of San Francisco. We at Finger's have endeavored to capture the nostalgia of those bygone days for all to once again enjoy."

And enjoy it folks did, making Finger's a longtime favorite. Entrées bore the names of plays. The fried chicken was called Yankee Doodle Dandy, steak and lobster Romeo and Juliet and the fried shrimp Madame Butterfly. Barbecued spareribs became, of course, Picnic, and so it went. One of the house drinks was the Red Garter, a delectable mixture of orange juice, lemon juice, tequila and grenadine. It was served with a souvenir red garter wrapped around the glass for the customer to keep. Each entrée had a recommended wine that included all the trendy choices of the day: Mateus (both white and rose), Cold Duck, Liebfraumilch and Lambrusco. A tree behind the building was called the Hanging Tree, but there seems to be no documentation as to why, so it was probably an obscure theatrical reference.

One puzzling note on the menu offered adults children's portions for an additional two dollars. Children under ten could order a child-sized portion of regular menu items for two dollars less. Why would an adult pay more to receive less when anything left on the plate could easily be taken home?

Finger's is still fondly remembered and for a lot more than the toilet flusher–activated fountains, impressive though they were.

GIBSON'S

The building in which Gibson's Restaurant was located has a long and convoluted history. The seventeen-room mansion was built in 1873 by Augustus Paddock, a Great Lakes ship captain. It is at 1033 Lake Drive, in what is now called the East Hills area. In 1892, lumber baron Melvin Clark bought the property and lived there with his wife, Emily. After their deaths, their daughter, Marguerite, lived in the mansion with her husband, Edmund Wurzburg, who founded Wurzburg's Department Store, a longtime Grand Rapids fixture. The property was later bought by Polish Franciscan fathers, who refurbished the then shabby estate and turned it into the St. Bernardine's Friary. It served as a mission and also a home to priests and brothers.

In 1983, it became the upscale Gibson's Restaurant. It was so named because the early resident Emily Clark resembled the fashionable Gibson Girls made famous by artist Charles Dana Gibson. Since 2005, the estate has been part of the Gilmore Collection of area restaurants and operates today as Mangiamo! The exclamation point in the name may be a bit off-putting, but that doesn't take away from the quality of the food, which just happens to be some of the best Italian fare available. Anywhere. Somewhere hidden in the many nooks and crannies of the estate is a lovely reminder of Emily Clark, a stained-glass window depicting a Gibson Girl. Like its predecessor, Mangiamo! exemplifies fine dining, but fine dining in a more casual atmosphere that includes outdoor dining.

LES IDEES

Number 55 Ionia, NW, has a long history of serving some of the city's best food in the downtown area, including the Boar's Head in the Morton House. In 1978, Les Idees moved into the space, bringing it a sophisticated French flair and, as would be expected in a fine French restaurant, an extensive wine list. The décor spoke of understated class with tasteful oil paintings, dark wood and soft lighting. Classical music enhanced the feeling that, yes, this was indeed a place that would work as well on the Left Bank in Paris as it does in Midwest America. Ambience, however enticing, means nothing if the food doesn't measure up. No worries on that count, as the varied menu included veal, seafood and beef, all enhanced with French sauces guaranteed to turn good into great and great into phenomenal.

Along with the day-to-day menu, the restaurant courted the theater crowd with special limited-time after-theater menus served for the duration of the play's local run. The *Sound of Music* edition showed "Preludium" cocktails and appetizers. The "Maria" was quiche (Lorraine or Nicoise), salad and beverage; the Captain was a steak served with sautéed mushrooms, pommes frittes, garlic bread and tomatoes provencal; An Ordinary Couple, a European picnic for two, consisted of two kinds of bread, salami, cheeses, fruit and a half liter of wine; and the Sound of Music was a burger, fries and beverage. The choices listed under "My Favorite Things"—chocolate mousse, Japanese fruit pie or cheesecake—would have been shoe-ins on almost anyone's list of favorite things.

SAVORY STREET

Savory Street on Twenty-eighth Street charmed guests with what passed for New Orleans décor, right down to a row of French Quarter shop façades to add instant ambience. Even those who believed that New Orleans looked like that should have become suspicious when the house specialties were served in cast-iron skillets. That seemed a tad more backwoods South than sophisticated Crescent City. The fancier the restaurant, the more attention paid to the presentation, and it is a safe bet that fabled, top-of-the-line New Orleans eatery Antoine's never placed a cast-iron skillet on a patron's table.

Before smoking became verboten, restaurants like Savory Street used matchbooks for advertising giveaways. *Author's collection.*

Dinners were accompanied by Dave Miller's Muscat Ramblers every Tuesday. The jazz at least rang true, and dining at Savory Street was a fun, if not authentic, Louisiana experience. Some patrons came after dinner to enjoy a pitcher of martinis and basket of deep-fried mushrooms along with the French Quarter–style music associated with Preservation Hall. Other bands performed on weekends.

Duba's

Bob Robotham has vivid memories of his uncle, a tough-as-nails retired military man who for several years had endured the brutality of a Japanese prisoner of war camp during World War II. Having gotten through that ordeal, one would think that no one would ever be able to intimidate him again. And no one did…except his wife. Every time she directed her ire at him, he snapped into peacekeeping mode and quickly reserved a table at Duba's for a kiss-and-make-up dinner. Almost makes you wonder if she went out of her way to find reasons to complain. Yes, Duba's really was that good.

A fine dining restaurant was not founder Ed E. Duba's original plan. In 1949, with partner Al Wenger, he opened the Rocket Bar and Cafeteria. The plan was to add a bowling alley to their Stocking Avenue location. Wenger was already in the bowling business, and Ed Duba had become an ardent bowler.

The partners got off to a slow start, in part because the first cook they hired could make only one thing really well, and that was chili. A new chef named Al Megas came on board and suggested adding a thick slice of prime rib on rye bread to their lunch menu. The sixty-five-cent sandwich was an immediate hit. Then, at the urging of the night chef, Al Menga's brother, Duba's became the first area restaurant with lobster tail on the menu. The restaurant was by then doing so well that Ed dropped the idea of a bowling alley. Reluctantly.

Ed Duba bought Al Wenger out, and the Stocking Street white-tablecloth restaurant, no longer a cafeteria, quickly became a top spot to order a superb steak or one of the excellent seafood options. In addition to the lobster, the charbroiled halibut was especially good and guaranteed to turn former fish haters into lifelong fans. This time, four of Ed Duba's seven children—sons Ed J., Mike and Tom and daughter Sandy—came on board to make it a family enterprise. Ed's wife, Rosalie, was initially not very happy with the idea of her kids working in a place that served alcohol. She came around when she saw the positive side of five Dubas working together and building a family business to be proud of.

They operated successfully until patrons began finding the downtown area a less attractive spot to dine. Parking was both difficult and expensive. Petty crime also made people more inclined to eat in the relative safety of the suburbs. In 1990, the Duba family went with the flow and relocated to a ten-acre lot on the East Beltline. There they continued grilling steaks to charred perfection on the outside, with tender, juicy centers. The seafood was still delectable whether fried crisp, broiled or, like the thick halibut and whitefish steaks, charbroiled.

Ed Duba Sr. died on December 8, 2003. Duba's Restaurant closed on September 17, 2005. The family had intended to sell Northpointe Bank six acres and retain the other four and the restaurant. Then Northpointe made them an offer too good to refuse and bought the whole parcel. Yet another area landmark was gone for good.

MAKE MINE A STEAK, PLEASE

Mother's sounds like a family diner, but in fact it was a fine dining restaurant. *Author's collection.*

Carnivores ruled in Grand Rapids in the last half of the twentieth century. Even though all the popular restaurants of the time served other dishes, steak was what most people thought of when anticipating a dinner out. This was the era that taught us that "real men don't eat quiche"—at least not in the company of other real men.

Patrons of Kennedy's in Ada had to drive a short distance from town to the scenic spot on the Grand River at 7587 East Fulton Road. The cocktail lounge gave guests a view of the quaint village of Ada. There were fireplaces in both the Town and Country dining room and the lounge. Along with the usual selections of steak, chicken and seafood, diners could order the specialty of the house, Michigolden duckling. The duck was believed to be glazed with a sauce made from Michigan golden delicious apples.

Mother's on Plainfield Avenue was yet another place to partake of a steak and enjoy a gin and tonic or two. It was the first choice of many northeast Grand Rapids residents back in the day when north was north and south was south and seldom the twain met. Buying local meant the neighborhood itself, not the city at large.

Restaurateur Win Schuler at one time had a half dozen eateries in southwest Michigan. In addition to Grand Rapids, there were restaurants

The last restaurant of another gone-but-not-forgotten southwest Michigan favorite, Win Schuler's, closed in the 1990s. *Author's collection.*

in Grand Haven, Marshall and St. Joseph. Along with all manner of great steaks, Schuler's was known for its cheese spread served with crackers and the steaming crab bites, favorite dinner appetizers or bar snacks depending on the time of day. Served up with ice-cold beer in a frosted mug, or any other beverage of choice, the combination was pure bliss. Once called Barcheeze, the spread is now known simply as Win Schuler's Original Cheddar and can be found in grocery store dairy aisles. It's as tasty as ever. Try it with garlic toast or bagel chips. Now, if only we could find those crab bites…

The Silver Cloud on Leonard Street in the West Side was a good date place, as it offered dining and dancing. It was owned by the Bronkema brothers. The patriotic Bronkemas took pride in honoring locals serving in the military during World War II with a large display of framed photographs. The live music sometimes included talent brought in from outside the area and once featured popular blues singer Big Time Sarah from Chicago.

Wyoming residents could always count on a pleasant experience when dining out at Dick's Fine Food, located at 3539 Division Avenue, just south of Thirty-sixth Street. This restaurant served three meals a day, and as late as the 1960s, it was still possible to pop in for a light breakfast of coffee and toast for only a quarter. That made it popular with those working in the neighborhood.

Many Grand Rapids residents have fond memories of dining and dancing at the Silver Cloud, shown here with a display of locals serving in the military overseas. The owners were the Bronkema brothers, George (left) and John. *Grand Rapids Public Library.*

During the dinner hour, Dick's Fine Food was indeed fine, and all the juicy steaks were served with a large pat of butter melting into the charred top. A combination of changing tastes, a changing neighborhood and insufficient parking signaled the end. Throw in competition from national steakhouse chains, as well as the local Brann's Restaurants chain, and Dick's was rendered obsolete. It tried a new location with ample parking and a new name (Dick's Galley), but it was too little too late. Dick's steaks received their final pats of butter in 2003.

Also in Wyoming, on the northwest corner of Twenty-eighth Street and Burlingame Avenue, was the Swiss Chalet, far more American than Swiss. It was a place to get a good steak, baked potato and salad. Lunches were good, too, but often slow. For those who had the time, it was worth the wait.

Then it began looking a bit past its prime. What had once passed for charm started looking seedy. Jerry Rutkoski, who then also owned the Beltline Bar, came to the rescue. He acquired the building, gave it a much-needed face-lift and named it Jerry's Roadhouse. The menu was updated but had enough steak and standard choices to satisfy fans of the Swiss Chalet. Many found the downstairs preferable to the main dining area. Named the Rathskeller, it dished up casual favorites like chili topped with melted cheese and raw onions. In both its incarnations, the bar was popular with those working in the area.

Grand Rapids boasted a number of other places to go out for a steak in the 1970s and '80s. In addition to Duba's and Brann's, there was Duck's on Michigan Avenue and Langeliere's (formerly Arbana's) on the West Side and Lako's Dry Dock—both downtown. Tony Lakos started his eatery on Monroe Avenue but later moved to Pearl Street near the Highway 131 Pearl Street exit. Another downtown possibility was Mr. Clark's Beefeater, where Shirley Cherokee performed regularly in the lounge.

CHAPTER 4

Casual but Still Fine

Restaurants have been an important part of the area's commercial enterprises since the furniture industry first put the city on the map. Before Detroit became the Motor City and Battle Creek called itself Cereal City, Grand Rapids was a one-industry town: Furniture City. Out-of-town buyers came to the furniture markets in droves, and every one of them needed a place to eat. The burgeoning furniture industry brought new residents as well as visitors. Some of the Dutch and other Europeans were skilled carvers or other craftsman, while many were laborers. All were drawn here by the abundance of jobs.

Every culture that locates in a new area brings its food; eventually, someone opens a restaurant. Grand Rapids' rise to culinary diversity came gradually. Not so long ago, Chinese was the city's only Asian option. Now one can indulge in Thai, Japanese, Korean, Cambodian—you name it. There are now Indian and Persian options, as well as cafés representing the dishes of many of the varied African cultures.

The first two Chinese cooks were brought to Grand Rapids to work in the Pantlind Hotel kitchen. They were Moy Dum, the chef, and Moy Lung, his assistant. Their food and the accompanying Chinese tea were served on imported Chinese tableware and became so popular with hotel guests that management decided to make the experiment a permanent part of the menu. That opened the door for Chinese restaurants. One of the first downtown was the Hong Ying Lo, and it did a brisk business from 1927 to 1931. It was an exotic experience at that time, as it was decorated with Chinese lanterns hanging from the ceiling and ornately carved Asian furnishings.

One of the city's first Chinese restaurants was the Hong Ying Lo, and it operated from 1927 to 1931. *Grand Rapids Public Library.*

SUN SAI GAI

Although there were and are a number of local Chinese restaurants, one stands out. Anyone who doubted the possibility of achieving the American Dream in the mid-1900s had only to talk with Chinese immigrant Alvin Chin to be convinced. Like most who left their homeland for the chance to live a better life, he arrived with little more than a positive attitude and a strong work ethic. In 1928, he left his home in the Kwang Tung province and sailed with his uncle to Seattle. He had no money and spoke no English.

Eventually, he worked his way across the country getting jobs in various Chinese restaurants, including one in Kentucky, where he became a partner. The problem there was that his partner refused to hire enough help. That left Alvin so busy that he later said the only time he ever got off work was when he needed a haircut.

When he acquired the restaurant he named Sun Sai Gai, which translates to "New Prosperity," he lived at 24½ South Division Avenue, just across the street from the restaurant at 19 South Division. His restaurant was open almost every day from lunchtime until midnight or later. The only day he closed was Monday, and even with those brutal hours, he sometimes felt he was letting people down. He closed for only two holidays per year, Thanksgiving and the Fourth of July. The rest of the time, Alvin Chin worked, doing what he loved—building up his business while listening to the Chinese opera music he played on an old record player.

It was a small place—only thirteen booths and eleven tables for eat-in customers—but that worked because a large portion of his business was takeout. He never put up with rowdy behavior or drunkenness and never hesitated to softly, but firmly, tell offenders they could either behave or leave. He believed that his customers deserved a pleasant environment in which to enjoy their food. He also understood the first truism of running a service business: if anyone has a bad experience, not only will they not come back, but they will also tell others about it. In his opinion, it all boiled down to respect; if he respected his clientele, they would respect him back. For the most part, that served him well.

Chinese lanterns were hung from a green ceiling that could only be described as bilious. Red-flecked wallpaper and brown paneling covered the walls. The crowning glory was a beautifully ornate French Provincial–style mirror. The antique was a gift from the last owner of the Cody Hotel, who gave it to Alvin before the building was razed. The Sun Sai Gai had first operated in the hotel building smack dab in the center of the city at Fulton and Division. It opened in 1940 and was called Chung King Café. Chin took a job as manager in 1942 and bought it in 1949 after the Internal Revenue Service seized it for back taxes owed by the original owner.

The whole Chin family was involved. Alvin's wife, Fay, managed the kitchen, and his son Kent spent many years working at the restaurant until he was old enough to go away to college and become a doctor. Daughter Judy and younger son Yum all put in time working for Dad before they, too, left for college.

Buying the restaurant required a giant leap of faith. Restaurants are always a gamble, as no other industry has a higher fail rate. For the owner, the hours are long and the pressure unyielding. Vacations? Seldom. Sick days? Only if there is someone trustworthy to step in. More often than not, that someone is a wife or other family member.

But it takes more than confidence to build a successful restaurant. Above all else, the food has to be good. That posed no problem for Alvin Chin. He never thought that "good" was good enough and always strived for "excellent." Most who dined there would say he succeeded, none more so than Don and Edith Herrema. The Herremas toured China for nearly a month after visiting a family member who had been teaching English in a Hong Kong school. As their son, Ben, told it, "Mom and Dad's first stop when they arrived home was the Sun Sai Gai because one of the things they had missed most while in China was good Chinese food. They didn't think China's Chinese food was as good as Alvin Chin's!"

Alvin was the kind of person who would have done well no matter where he ended up because, in his mind, anything else was unacceptable. Local Chinese food aficionados felt blessed that he landed in Grand Rapids. He loved his Chinese music and made his living selling Chinese food, but he never regretted leaving China. Remembering what he had left made him all the more grateful for his new life in Michigan. "I'm American," he always said. "Those Commies are no good."

Sometimes people needed to get out and have a good meal but didn't want to dress up and make a big deal of it. After spending all day in business garb, chilling out sounded like a better option. Grand Rapids had plenty of choices even before the whole country devolved into full-time "Casual Friday" mode. In its day, the Colony House offered some of the best, but it was overshadowed as more and more competition crept into the downtown area. It still remained a favorite place to gather for a quiet meeting with old colleagues, as General William Covell did with his World War II Company H friends in 1947.

A deep bond exists between people who have shared the horrors of war. General William Covell (seated, center) meets with a few of his World War II Company H colleagues at the Colony House in 1947. *Grand Rapids Public Library.*

The serving staff at the Colony House, looking crisp, clean and ready for work. *Grand Rapids Public Library.*

In December 1948, the Colony House had a full-page "Season's Greetings" ad in the *Grand Rapids Herald.* In it were images of the employees, the building's exterior and interiors of the Grill Room, the Marine Room and the Main Dining Room. Management hoped to remind readers that they still had private dining rooms, were able to cater large affairs and that the everyday menu included delectable entrées of steaks, seafood, lobster, mutton chops and frogs' legs. And unlike many fine food establishments, the Colony House also served breakfast and lunch.

THE BRANN FAMILY RESTAURANTS

Although the Brann family's local chain of steakhouses officially began in 1960 when John Brann opened a restaurant on Division Avenue in Burton Heights, the family name has been associated with good food since the 1930s, when John's brother, Tom, started the Porterhouse on Division Avenue and Oakes Street. There was a reason many thought it the best steakhouse in the Midwest: Tom Brann selected, trimmed and cured all the beef he served. It was fine dining, to be sure. A relish tray came first, followed by soup or salad. After that came the main event: a steak done to sizzling perfection—whether a lady's cut petite filet mignon or the namesake porterhouse, it never disappointed.

Drinks were mixed to perfection, and the beer was frosty. There was a separate Stag Bar, a popular spot for men to gather. When Tom Brann died, his widow, Millie, and brother, John, tried to keep the Porterhouse going, but it was too much for her and John had his hands full with his own Brann Restaurants that he and his sons operated.

That, along with heightened competition for evening business and the changing neighborhood, forced the Porterhouse to close in 1975. That portion of Division Avenue had become the playground of prostitutes and a clientele that preferred sleazy bars over some of the best food in the city. Even the most loyal Porterhouse patrons no longer felt comfortable there after dark.

The Stag Bar was part of the first Brann restaurant, the Porterhouse, and enjoyed a long run downtown on Division Avenue. *Grand Rapids Public Library.*

John Brann introduced the Sizzler, cut from the tri tip in 1967, and a legend was born. Soon Brann's was serving about eight hundred of the west Michigan specialties on Saturdays. John Brann's place also eventually closed, but the other Brann's Restaurants are going strong (eleven in 2015). Although the Porterhouse and the earlier Brann's Restaurants were considered fine dining, the ambience has grown more casual over the years. The corporate website describes the eateries as "a casual dining restaurant in a sports bar disguise."

The atmosphere may have chilled out, but two things that remain unchanged are the excellent steaks and the public's demand for them. Johnny Brann Jr., grandson of John Brann, got into the family business in 2013 with his own restaurant, a bistro he named Kitchen 67, or K67. It is located on the East Beltline, and the "67" in the name is a nod to the year his grandfather introduced the famous Sizzler to a town that has always known how to appreciate it.

Tommy Brann is the current president of the Brann's organization, and if pure dedication is a criterion, there could be no better choice. He became owner of Tommy Brann's, located at 4157 South Division Avenue, a few miles south of his father's Burton Heights restaurant, when he was only nineteen. John Brann knew that the shuttered Southern Bar-B-Q was up for sale and made an impulsive decision to lend his son money to buy it rather than send him to college to learn—what else?—restaurant management.

Tommy met his wife, Sue, when she took a job waitressing for him. That came as no surprise to anyone who knew him. Of course he met Sue at Tommy Brann's. He never went anywhere else! Thirty-plus years later, he still doesn't. The poster child for successful hands-on ownership, Brann is there every day, from opening to closing, living up to his slogan: "Wears Apron, Loves to Serve." On any given day, he can be found grilling Sizzlers, replenishing the salad bar, busing tables and mopping floors. And with all that, he is never too busy to find the time for what he enjoys most: greeting and talking with his guests.

He has always been more than the name on the door. He *is* Tommy Brann's and savors every minute of it. The only thing he might have learned in a college restaurant management program that he doesn't already know is how to delegate. It wouldn't have made any difference, as delegation is simply not in his nature. Maybe that is why national steakhouse chains come and go in Grand Rapids, while the local chain, Brann's, just keeps sizzling on.

Several generations of Grand Rapidians remember one of the Brann's Restaurants as the place they went on the first date with their future spouse. Some became engaged there and, like Morrie and Jane Bylsma, continue to celebrate their anniversaries there, though now it's with children and grandchildren in tow. "We started at John Brann's and really hated to see it close," Jane said. "We knew all the waitresses. We knew John." Like his son, John Brann recognized the importance of being both visible and approachable.

Jane said that in all the years they went there, they kept to a routine. "We always went in through the back door, and we always ordered the same thing. A kebob for Morrie. A Sizzler for me," she said, "Now we go to Tommy Brann's, and after the first couple of times we felt as much at home as we did at his dad's place. Tommy goes out of his way to make sure you do."

Der Kelder

In the late summer of 1967, then Morton House owners Jerry and Millie Houting opened a new restaurant in the building and named it Der Kelder, meaning "The Cellar" in Dutch. The Old World–style dining hall specialized in serving Dutch and German favorites, including knockwurst, bratwurst, pig hocks and sauerkraut, all washed down with schnapps and "bier." Diners ate under the watchful eye of Piet Hien, a sixteenth-century Dutch sea captain and privateer during the Eighty Years' War between the United Provinces and Spain.

The Houtings' Piet Hien was fashioned from a mannequin dressed in a costume and sporting an oversized nose along with a shock of unruly blond hair. Piet was positioned to look as if he were working the galley table in front of the hams, bologna rings and other meats. The Piet Hien Special consisted of three meats, sauerkraut, German potato salad and a dense, dark rye bread. Viennese waltzes played in the background. The Dutch Piet Hien is often confused with his direct descendant, a Dane also named Piet Hien. The Danish namesake was well known for writing short, aphoristic verses called "Grooks," which were often quoted by restaurant guests. They could almost be described as nursery rhymes for adults, and one of the restaurant favorites was:

Meeting the Eye
You'll probably find that it suits your book,
to be a bit cleverer than you look.
And the simplest way to do this by far,
is to look a bit stupider than you are.

Der Kelder replaced the previous Morton House bar and restaurant, the Kitten Club, Grand Rapids' watered-down version of the Playboy Clubs. Watered down or not, it was thought racy for the time. Especially eyebrow raising was how the club's waitstaff was made up entirely of attractive young women who were called kittens and wore high heels, bustiers and cat ears.

One of those kittens garnered nationwide attention when she was outed as a thirty-seven-year-old cat with ten kitties of her own. Men felt cheated, and women were jealous because she had been able to pull it off. She had taken the job when her husband lost his job and the family needed money. No one could blame her for choosing to work in the club, as there was nowhere else in town where she could earn as much money and still be home with her children during the day. Unsavory though they might have seemed to the more uptight of the local residents, the Grand Rapids kittens were mild compared to Playboy Bunnies.

In 1970, the Morton House filed for bankruptcy. The Saperstein family bought the building and converted it to low-cost apartments but continued leasing space to restaurants like Les Idees, which came onboard a few years later.

Bill's Place: Where a Young Man Learned a Huge Secret

We can only guess at what secrets are buried deep within a restaurant's walls. Sometimes the one who carries the secret simply comes by unannounced and drops a bombshell. As an adult, former president Gerald R. Ford Jr. was the Grand Rapids manifestation of "local boy does good." But that all happened long after the then seventeen-year-old junior at South High School took a part-time job at Bill's Place. The restaurant was owned by Bill Skougis and was located across Hall Street from the school.

Its location made it a natural teen gathering spot, and the eatery served diner-style food and locally made Hoekstra ice cream. Bill Skougis was a big South High School football fan and loved hiring members of the team. For two dollars a week plus lunch, young Jerry Ford washed dishes, served food and worked the cash register. He was the eldest of Gerald Sr. and Dorothy Ford's four sons.

He knew that his mother had been previously married and divorced. He even knew that Gerald Sr. was not his biological father. What he didn't know was anything at all about Dorothy Ford's former husband, an Omaha, Nebraska businessman named Leslie Lynch King. On their honeymoon, King physically abused his new bride, and she realized that she had made a huge mistake.

Even though the abuse continued, Dorothy decided against divorce when she realized she was pregnant. Two weeks after the arrival of a boy named Leslie Lynch King Jr., Dorothy King fled Nebraska. By then she was afraid that King would also hurt her child. She took young Leslie to Harvard, Illinois, where her parents lived, and never looked back. Later, the family moved to Grand Rapids, where Dorothy met Gerald Ford, a Grand Rapids paint salesman for the family business Ford Paint and Varnish. The couple married when Leslie was three. Gerald Ford adopted the boy and changed his name to Gerald Ford Jr.

Fast-forward fourteen years. Leslie King Sr. had found out enough about his biological son to be impressed with his athletic prowess and wanted to have a relationship. He even hoped that Jerry would come and live with him and his new family in Riverton, Wyoming. King had also left Omaha, but for reasons that spoke directly to his character: escaping the long arm of the law to avoid paying Nebraska court–ordered child support to Dorothy. Money was never the real issue, as King came from a wealthy family and could have easily have made the payments. Instead, he decided that no judge was going to tell him what to do and relocated outside the Nebraska court's jurisdiction.

One can only imagine the shock Jerry Ford must have felt on that Michigan day in 1930 when a stranger came in to Bill's Place and asked him if he was Leslie King. When he said no, the man asked if he was Gerald Ford. He answered that question with a yes, and the stranger made a mind-boggling announcement: "You are Leslie King, and I am your father. I'd like to take you to lunch and talk."

Ford asked Bill for permission to leave the restaurant, and the two went outside. Jerry met King's second wife, and they all went to the Cherie Inn for lunch. He later said that he was shocked, confused and angry. Despite that, he pulled himself together and made it clear that he was happy in his tightknit family and had no interest in leaving Gerald Ford Sr., the man he loved and respected and who was the only father he had ever known.

That night, he learned the whole story, and the next day his three brothers were told. He put the whole episode behind him, as it was common in those days not to talk about adoption details. He saw King a few more times over the years and met his half brother and two half sisters. Communications were cordial, but no one ever doubted that Jerry was a Ford and proud of it.

As for Bill's Place, it is long gone, leaving us to wonder what other secrets it might have harbored and if any could possibly have been as dramatic as that one.

Lanning's Restaurant and Catering

Lanning's Restaurant and Catering at 433 West Leonard Street in the Creston neighborhood had a loyal following since 1941, when the original owner, Roscoe Lanning, opened it under the name Humpty Dumpty. By the 1950s, Lanning was delivering chicken dinners all over town. His operating mantra was "Giving great food at a family affordable price." Although the restaurant was known for its chicken dinners, the menu featured items not found everywhere else, like Buttercrumb Scrod and liver and onions. Steaks and sandwiches were always good choices as well.

Roscoe changed the name to Lanning's, but the reputation remained intact, and the company branched out into catering. It provided full china place settings and linen tablecloths at no additional cost and took great pride in being chosen to cater weddings for the daughters of couples whose weddings they had catered a quarter of a century earlier.

The Lanning family retired from the business, and the new owners, Pete and Denny Mink, were running the show when the restaurant finally had to close its doors in 2010. Like so many other neighborhood treasures, they were unable to compete with the ever-growing number of chains staking claims in the suburbs.

The Three Crowns

The Three Crowns was located downtown on Monroe Mall, at that time a pedestrian-only, two-block shopping and dining mecca. It specialized in European fare, but from four, not three, countries. Among other selections, the menu offered Swedish smorgasbord, quiche Lorraine from France, German-style beef stroganoff and Italian lasagna. It had a separate menu for "Ladies and Gentlemen under 12."

When the downtown department stores moved to suburban malls, the smaller shops followed. Most of the restaurants, Three Crowns included, were forced to close. Relocating was not a viable option, as it would have been unable to compete with the multitude of places to eat both inside the malls and in the surrounding area.

GRANNY'S KITCHEN

Granny's Kitchen is remembered fondly for its early American style, which did indeed resemble granny's kitchens, or at least our romanticized idea of how they should have looked. A train looping below the ceiling provided more charm. Most memorable, though, were the cute teenage girls rocking in an oversized rocking chair on an elevated platform in front of the building. They wore granny costumes and waved to one and all. It was a good gig. In the 1970s, the girls received seven dollars per hour for a three-hour shift.

Inside, diners ordered everything from a Platter-O-Pancakes to Grand Pappy's Hillbilly Fried Chicken. Until the 1980s, it held the distinction of being one of a very few eateries to open on major holidays, including Christmas.

Through all his years in Washington as a congressman representing the district that includes Grand Rapids, Gerald R. Ford, with his wife, the former Betty Bloomer, returned home to vote on election day. Their tradition, after leaving the voting booth, was to head to Granny's Kitchen for breakfast. It usually involved speaking with a few friends and well-wishers before tucking into some of the area's best pancakes. On election day, November 2, 1976,

President Gerald R. Ford on election day in 1976, outside Granny's Restaurant, where he and Betty always went for breakfast after voting. *Gerald R. Ford Presidential Library.*

The president signs the restaurant guest book while First Lady Betty Ford looks on. Stopping at Granny's was a tradition going back to Ford's time representing the area in Michigan's Third Congressional District. *Gerald R. Ford Presidential Library.*

while he was president, it was more like a mob scene. The Fords graciously greeted the assembled media and spoke to as many locals as time allowed.

LEONARD STREET MARKET

Akin to Granny's Kitchen in ambience was the Leonard Street Market. Opened by Marc and Tom DeMaat on Leonard Street NW, just west of downtown, this eatery also harkened back to a slower time. The former interurban depot was sandblasted and renovated inside to house a deli, an ice cream parlor, a pie shop and a general bakery. All that and a restaurant, too.

The restaurant served tasty home-style soups, sandwiches and salads, along with specials like perfectly breaded, buttery Boston scrod. The soups were all made from fresh ingredients that were often bought from the produce market next door. The Canadian cheese soup was the favorite of many and said to be the best in town. Another popular soup choice was vegetable meatball. Pea soup made the Dutch way, with mettwurst, was great alongside an Uncle Rueben sandwich. The menu was peppered with hokey names like Whistle Wetters for the drinks and sandwiches called the City Slicker, Cousin Homer and Fat Albert, to name a few. It wasn't unusual for diners to order a slice of fruit pie for dessert and then take home a whole pie from Aunt Maggie's Pie Shop.

The whole thing was set among antiques and quaint finds, including an old soda fountain and coffee grinder. Servers wore charming old-fashioned garb, and the walls were papered in an early American pattern. The Leonard Street Market was eventually acquired by Arnie's Bakery and Restaurants.

H&L SANDWICH SHOP

The December 17, 1929 *Grand Rapids Herald* ran an article on the downtown H&L Sandwich Shop, proclaiming it the city's most popular eating place. Located at 127 Ottawa Avenue, across from the Michigan Trust Building, it was one of the few offering twenty-four-hour service. It was owned and operated by Don Hunting, and the character of the place could best be described as folksy. A sign reinforced it: "Tipping is a gratuity from a superior to an inferior. We're just a bunch of American boys. Please don't insult us."

Hunting never had delusions of what his business was all about. By limiting menu items to sandwiches, salads, breakfast selections and desserts,

Some thought that the downtown H&L Sandwich Shop, shown here in 1935, was the best in town. *Grand Rapids Public Museum.*

he could do an outstanding job on the items he chose to serve. He scrambled his eggs with cream, and all his pies were made from scratch. One thing he was known for was his toasted rolls, a tradition going back to his University of Michigan student days in Ann Arbor. The M, coffee or milk with toasted rolls, was the usual daily breakfast for the college kids burdened with 8:00 a.m. classes. To the delight of Michigan alumni and fans, another restaurant sign noted, "We have the M."

On the day of the *Herald* article, Hunting was offering free Maxwell House coffee. It was the only coffee he ever served, and he was participating with the coffee company in a special promotion. That, too, was part of the Hunting philosophy of serving the best of good old-fashioned American diner food and drink. Had there been Starbucks coffee back then, his customers would neither have needed it nor wanted it.

BILL KNAPP'S

Bill Knapp's, once a thriving local chain, is still missed. *Author's collection.*

Bill Knapp's was a local chain starting in Kalamazoo, with two eateries in Grand Rapids that thrived for four decades. It lived up to its slogan, "A meal or a snack," and was greatly missed when the last Grand Rapids facility closed in 1987, depriving diners of crowd pleasers that included ham croquettes, potatoes au gratin and a sundae built on a dense chocolate cake base.

All the restaurants looked alike, and the entryway featured an oversized, semicircular bench on which to sit while waiting for a booth. It could be a long wait on weekends. One regular occurrence was a tinny-sounding recording of "Happy Birthday." Being singled out with that less-than-melodious attention was probably enjoyed by some, while it made others cringe. Neal Southworth remembered it well: "The only way I would have gone to Bill Knapp's on my birthday would have been if someone held a gun to my head."

Choices on the children's menu were named for animals. The Giraffe was a grilled cheese sandwich, the Zebra was a fried chicken drumstick with French fries and a biscuit and the Lion was a steak burger. There were a few other choices, and all were served with milk, hot chocolate or Coke, as well as applesauce, pears or ice cream for dessert.

Proof of Bill Knapp's iconic status in Michigan came in early 2015 when a booth rescued from a Knapp's building that was to be razed appeared on the TruTV Channel's *Hardcore Pawn* reality series. The show is filmed in Detroit at the American Jewelry and Loan pawnshop and is more about the confrontational weirdos who parade in and out than about merchandise bought and sold. Store patriarch Les Gold bought the booth for $200 and then quickly flipped it to an antique shop owner for $325. Michiganders statewide still miss having "a meal or a snack" at Bill Knapp's.

BOSTON HOUSE FAMILY RESTAURANT

The Boston House dated back to the mid-1800s, and the former stagecoach stop stayed in operation for about one hundred years. A company logo of a coach being pulled by a team of four horses paid tribute to its humble past. Set in the Boston Square neighborhood that grew up around it, the roadhouse turned restaurant at 1353 Kalamazoo Avenue was a fixture. It probably originally served the Grand Rapids–Kalamazoo Line that operated on the Kalamazoo Plank Road.

"When I was growing up there [in the Boston Square neighborhood], my dad told stories of an eccentric relative who sort of worked there when it was still a stage stop," said Connie VanAtta, who lived in Boston Square most of her life. "I say 'sort of' because Bertie had a problem with the bottle. He'd go off on a bender, then find his way back there and muck out stalls and feed and water horses in exchange for food. Guess he slept in the stable. Dad said he smelled like he did." She went on to say that Bertie would sober up for a time and then repeat the process.

When motorized vehicles rendered stagecoaches obsolete, the restaurant made a seamless transition into modern-day life. Sandwiches reflected the name of the neighborhood with items like the Boston Bird (turkey), Boston Square (beef, ham and cheese) and Boston House Philly. One could indulge in a Big Boston Breakfast of eggs, a choice of meat that included Polish sausage, potatoes and toast. A mini version on the kids' menu was called BBB, or Boston House Breakfast Bonanza.

It was a typical neighborhood establishment where most patrons were regulars who lived or worked in the area, and meals were accompanied by the comfortable hum of table-to-table chatter not often heard in an IHOP.

MR. STEAK

There were two Mr. Steaks in the area, one on Plainfield Avenue and the other on Twenty-eighth Street in Wyoming. The food was tasty and inexpensive, a hard combination to beat. Steaks were small but tender, the salads crisp and the bread fresh-baked. Rhonda Ayers of Jenison remembered working at the Twenty-eighth Street restaurant in the early 1980s. "It was just a good place to work," she recalled. "The manager was nice, and so were most of the customers." During the lunch-hour rush, her mother's friends always asked to be seated in her section because they knew she would get them served and out so they could get back to work on time. The patrons she labeled "not so nice" were the vendors from the weekend flea market, who made a practice of not tipping the servers.

LITTLE MEXICO CAFÉ

Mexican restaurants have always had a loyal following, and not just in the Hispanic community. Martin Morales bought the Little Mexico Café in 1972. The northwest corner of Bridge Street and Stocking Avenue restaurant soon became a West Side icon and grew to employ more than twenty-five workers. Morales hailed not from Mexico but from Rio Grande City, Texas. He was larger than life and become known for the shenanigans he pulled in his ongoing efforts to improve the lives of those in his community. One event involved riding a horse into city hall when he failed to get attention in more conventional ways. He was stopped before making much progress, but as a publicity stunt, it was a home run.

Always active in local politics, he even ran for mayor. He lost the election, but in the end, he probably accomplished more through his activism than he ever could have as an insider. Not bad for a man who left home at age nine with only a third-grade education. His family was dirt poor, and he figured that if he left, there would be one less mouth to feed.

Little Mexico was decorated in a Mayan theme, and the murals were painted by local artist William Bouwsema. The finished product was bold and colorful, much like Martin Morales himself. Although he was known for raging like a rutting moose when he felt he needed to draw attention to a cause, Martin admitted to having a bigger bark than bite. A perfect example was when he stormed out of a dinner honoring retiring mayor Abe Drasin. It seems that Morales had hired a Mexican mariachi band as part of the entertainment, but when the musicians arrived late, the event organizer, Pete Secchia, told them they couldn't play. The next day, Morales told the press that Secchia's behavior had been a deliberate slap in the face to all the area Latinos.

Secchia was puzzled by such a confrontational attitude from someone with whom he thought he had an amiable relationship despite their political differences. When he stopped at the Little Mexico Café on a peacemaking mission, Martin greeted him with an affable smile. "Pablo, the only time I get my name in the paper is when I fight with you," he said. That was as close as he could bring himself to apologize without fear of losing face. He led Secchia to the bar and poured him a drink.

Martin Morales's my-way-or-the-highway political stances made him revered in the Latino community. His expertise in serving Mexican food made him revered in the area at large. Some say, and probably Martin himself would agree, that the Little Mexico created the Grand Rapids specialty, the wet burrito, but that honor goes to the Beltline Bar when it was still owned by Jerry Rutkowski. It was the happy result of a delivery error.

Martin continued operating the Little Mexico and ruffling feathers in city hall until 1999, when legal woes, including illegal drug trafficking in the building, along with financial difficulties, forced him into bankruptcy. Long after he had hung up his apron and retired, local government leaders often called on him for consultations on Hispanic issues. No longer an object of ridicule, he cared deeply about his people, and the city fathers were finally willing to listen.

Enrique and Consuela Ayala bought the eatery from Martin and operated it for fourteen years before closing it in 2013. New ownership did not lessen the restaurant's popularity, and the couple did well initially. Even a devastating fire in September 2008 slowed but failed to stop them.

Martin Morales's beloved murals were destroyed in that fire. In their place, Roland Mancera painted new ones, this time with Aztec art replacing the Mayan. On reopening day, February 12, 2010, a long line waited to chow down on beloved Tex-Mex chimichangas, chile rellenos, tacos, burritos and enchiladas. Even those who had to wait in line for an hour or more for a table agreed that it was worth the wait.

The Little Mexico Café was closed for good in 2014, largely due to insurmountable financial issues. The West Side neighborhood mourned another lost landmark.

Peter Secchia, Morales's "frenemy," was a restaurateur in his own right. Long a major player in the local business community and beyond, Secchia opened Pietro's in 1980 to honor the long history of fine Italian dining that he had enjoyed in the home of his grandparents, Pietro and Regina Secchia.

Pietro's is still going strong and prepares everything from scratch, even the croutons, pastas and salad dressings. Dishes are matched with the perfect wines. Regina's legendary kitchen lives on, now for all to enjoy. This is a place that might evoke memories of feasts that occurred regularly and were interwoven with large portions of family love and lore. It might, but only if you were lucky enough to be born into a large, loving family with roots in Italy. Pietro's continues the Secchia family generosity as well. One of the ways it does that is by providing free Thanksgiving dinners, with all the traditional sides, at the local Mel Trotter Mission. *Bravissimo!*

Secchia also brought Tootsie Van Kelly's saloon to the Amway Grand Plaza Hotel. Tootsie's was named for a singer and dancer in the Phoenix, Arizona area named Ruth Russell. Her stage name was Tootsie Van Kelly, and she was also known as Red Hot Mama. She died in Grand Rapids on October 15, 2007, at age seventy-eight. Secchia rose to political prominence when President Ford appointed him ambassador to Italy.

THE ONION CROCK

Introduced in 1974, the Onion Crock had three restaurants: at 1508 Wealthy Street, North Kent Mall and downtown at 116 Monroe. Beginning with soups, salads, sandwiches and home-baked pies, it gradually added more to the menu. But if you ask people what they miss most about the Onion Crock, it's a good bet that the answer will be soup—specifically French onion soup. It was quite simply the best in town. Starting with a crock of rich beef broth and onions, the soup was then topped with the eatery's own croutons. Next came three different kinds of cheese on the croutons, and then the whole thing was baked under the broiler. The melted cheese turned into a glorious stringy mess that was hard to eat while retaining any dignity. Folks asked for extra napkins and dug in with gusto.

Not that the other soups weren't good. They were. Country clam chowder (Manhattan or New England style), minestrone, Wisconsin cheese—any one of the fifty soups with a sandwich and/or a crisp salad drizzled with one of the four Onion Crock dressings were guaranteed to bring customers back for more. Except for the signature French onion, not every soup was available every day.

The restaurants were named for the crocks the onion soup was baked in, as well as the crocks of scallions and pickles that patrons munched while waiting for their lunch. The closing of the Onion Crocks a few years later left a city craving French onion soup. Fortunately, those cravings can be satisfied, as a few specialty grocers stock the most popular of the soups. Look for it in the freezer case.

Kegler's Sundowner's

If you think the only food you can get in a bowling alley is packaged chips or nuked sandwiches, it's clear that you have never experienced Sundowner's in the Eastbrook Lanes. Kegler's was the lounge, and Sundowner's served up full dinners of steaks, shrimp and other seafood. Most entrées included the salad bar; French fries, steak fries or a baked potato; and buttery garlic bread. Lighter choices were Chef Jack's Denver Great Omelette or a wide selection of sandwiches, the most popular of which were Kegler's Highstacker (French dip), the Atlantic Submarine or the signature Keglerburger Plate.

Many stopped for dinner on bowling night or for a late-night supper after bowling. But for some, the allure was not the lanes but the lounge. They have warm memories of stopping in Kegler's Lounge, sipping a Harvey Wallbanger or two and dancing to the honeyed voice of the ever-lovely Geri Bek. Simply hearing a few bars of "Our Day Will Come" or "Yesterday," they are back in that cozy night spot dancing in the arms of someone they once loved. Or, if they're lucky, someone they still do.

On South Division Avenue

South Division had multiple drive-ins and cafés serving up great food that fell out of favor when McDonald's came along and proved that it could do it faster. Sprinkled in the mix were a few that offered a lot more. In addition to the Log Cabin and Dick's Fine Food mentioned elsewhere, there were two longtime favorites: the Southern Bar-B-Q and the Hickory Bar-B-Q.

Anyone thinking that barbecue could be found only south of the Mason-Dixon line during the middle of the twentieth century would quickly learn otherwise while cruising South Division Avenue. A disproportionate number of eateries added "Bar-B-Q" to their names. The Midwest version of barbecue almost always referred to barbecued beef or pork ribs and was a far cry from a typical southern pig-pickin' feast or the beloved pulled or sliced pork sandwich topped with vinegary coleslaw and served on soft buns or Kaiser rolls. Midwest barbecue tasted good, too, but it was definitely different.

The Southern Bar-B-Q, not to be confused with the Southland Tavern on the east side of Twenty-eighth Street, was founded by A.S. Beals at the site now occupied by Tommy Brann's. (Yes, the sign simply says Brann's, but to a few generations of die-hards, it is and always will be Tommy Brann's.) The four white pillars out front, not the menu, probably inspired the name. It wasn't Tara, but it had a charm all its own. Because there were a few cabins on the property, the Southern also called itself a motel and advertised the dwellings as modern and heated.

A complete dinner of steak, seafood, barbecued ribs or fried chicken, washed down by a cocktail or two, made for pleasant dining. One thing that separated it from most of the other barbecue competition was a larger selection of seafood choices, unusual during the time before refrigerated rail cars and delivery trucks made serving seafood easy. Beals also served frogs' legs. Throw in a background of mellow tunes emanating from the Hammond organ and you have romantic dining. It proved so popular that less than six years after opening, the owners expanded, as they were serving twenty times as many people.

Weekends always meant a dance band playing toe-tapping favorites that encouraged even the most reluctant diners to grab a partner and shake a leg. One of those dance bands was the Smoothies, who promised soothing music for dancing. This was well before rock-and-roll came along, and the words *music* and *soothing* were seldom used in the same sentence. Couples weren't expected to dance like Fred and Ginger, just to get up and have fun.

By the 1940s, the restaurant was managed by Herb and Esther Keyser, who lived in a nearby cabin. When the restaurant went up for sale, John Brann bought it for his son, Tommy.

The Hickory Bar-B-Q's claim to fame was its broiled steaks. One reason for that was owner Nick Daniels's specially built broiler. It had two extra-large trays with removable grills and enabled him to broil one hundred streaks at a time. That wasn't usually an issue, but the restaurant's Club Room could seat from 20 to 120 people for private parties.

He also did a bang-up job of coming up with ideas guaranteed to increase traffic. One of his best attention-grabbers occurred when he invited Santa Claus to stop at the Hickory on at least one Christmas Eve afternoon.

Mellow music to dine by was standard at the Southern Bar-B-Q during the week, with dance bands on weekends. *Grand Rapids Public Library.*

Despite it being his busiest day of the whole year, the jolly gent accepted. For two hours, Santa treated children to ice cream and their parents to coffee and doughnuts. He managed to save a little time by showing up in his red suit so he wouldn't have to change clothes before harnessing the reindeer for his long night of worldwide deliveries.

Daniels opened on Christmas Day for limited hours and cooked up a special holiday dinner in lieu of his regular menu. He was one of the first in the area to think of those without nearby family with whom to celebrate or those traveling through town looking for more than junk food from one of the few open gas stations.

TAVERNS

Taverns have traditionally been more than drinking establishments and were more like the British pubs where simple food was served and where people gathered to socialize. In this country, those people were often immigrants who enjoyed being with their fellow countrymen. Christian Schmitt operated a popular tavern on the northwest corner of Burton Street and Godfrey Avenue that was largely frequented by Germans. The Schmitt family started its American odyssey in California during the gold rush, and the next generation found its way to Grand Rapids.

Not everyone can claim to have had their beer served by a dog, and if they did, the assumption would probably be that they had indulged in a little too much of that beer. Not among the Lithuanian immigrants, most of whom

Christian Schmitt presides over his saloon on the northeast corner of Burton Street and Godfrey Avenue in about 1900. *Grand Rapids Public Museum.*

When Spooky wasn't mugging for the camera or barking in time to the music from the piano, he served beer in his owner's tavern. *Grand Rapids Public Library.*

were hardworking, blue-collar Catholics living in the West Side. Like every other group settling here, they had their favorite go-to eateries, including the restaurant and tavern owned by John Sabaitis on the southeast corner of Muskegon and Richmond.

A case could be made that the real draw was a German shepherd named Spooky that could both entertain and serve beer. Sabaitis made a carrier for the dog to wear so he could deliver beers to patrons seated at tables. He waited tables only when he wasn't busy accompanying the piano player with his lusty barks. The picture of Spooky was posed, as he would not have been allowed to drink on the job. At some point, either John or the health department forced Spooky's retirement.

GRABBING A QUICK BITE

For a long time, downtown workers and shoppers could lunch at counters in many of the downtown retail establishments. The ones in the department stores were usually called coffee shops, and stores like Herpolshimer's, Wurzburg's and Steketee's also had tearooms or other spots for lunch with a bit more panache. People with a one-hour or less lunch break preferred counters in dime stores or drugstores that also had soda fountains. Soda fountains had a long reign of popularity, going all the way back to the fountain at West's Drugs and its refreshing pineapple ice.

Many considered Kresge's the best of the bunch. It was definitely the biggest, and the 1936 menu boasted "a good cup of coffee served with pure cream" for only seven cents. Cokes were a better bargain at a nickel. Diners sat on red swivel stools at a marble counter. Ah, the luxury!

The Banquet Bar-B-Q was a longtime downtown favorite, noted for its good food and attentive service. It was a no-frills spot for a quick meal of a sandwich or a full plate lunch. The sodas and malts were always winners.

Another favorite lunch-on-the-run spot was the Twentieth Century Café, where service was quick and efficient. Add good food to the equation and it's easy to see why most of the stools at the counter were filled during the busier times of the day.

Mid-twentieth-century ladies who lunched sometimes upped the fun quotient by attending special events, like this fashion show held at Herpolshimer's Department Store. *Grand Rapids Public Library.*

The soda fountain in West's Drug Store was noted for its ornate carved and painted bar. *Grand Rapids Public Library.*

The popular Banquet Bar-B-Q had a large crew, but this picture seems to have been taken during a slower time. *Grand Rapids Public Library.*

The exterior of the popular Banquet Bar-B-Q in 1937. *Grand Rapids Public Library.*

Bowling alleys usually had lunch counters in the early days, and like the one at Northfield Lanes, they were fast, economical and comfortable. Diners could drop in for a quick meal even when not bowling. The one in the image on page 80 is typical, right down to the round stools, watchful waitress and the glass dessert display case. Those cases were seen everywhere and almost always contained a few slices of Boston cream pie.

Blue-plate specials were daily offerings at low prices and included meat and two or three sides, all served on one divided blue plate. No substitutions allowed. They were found in most cafés, diners and lunch counters. Some say that Fred Harvey started the trend in the late 1800s in his Harvey Houses. Others claim that the Atlantic Seaboard Railroad was first in 1915. The specials became popular during the Great Depression and lasted through the 1950s.

Wednesday's 1939 blue-plate special at Peck's Drug Store was meatloaf with gravy, mashed potatoes, green peas and a dinner roll with one pat of butter. It set a customer back fifty-five cents, unless he or she ordered coffee. That raised the tab an extra nickel.

Everyone benefited from the specials. The win/win plates allowed diners to eat reasonably priced meals and gave the restaurant the chance to use up extra supplies of foods before they spoiled. It even saved on manpower, with fewer dishes to wash back in the day when that kind of labor was done by people with their arms elbow deep in dishwater. As time went on, some establishments used disposable plates, still blue, that were the forerunners of TV dinner trays.

Of all the lunch counters, Peck's Drug Store is the most remembered, and not for its superior tuna salad sandwiches on toasted white bread served with chips and a pickle. Peck's notoriety stems from two murders. In 1915, Arthur Waite, a New York doctor originally from Grand Rapids, married Clara Louise Peck, daughter of a wealthy pharmacist, John E. Peck. Not long after the wedding, Arthur put into motion a devious plan to acquire the Peck family fortune. Clara's mother visited the newlyweds the following January, during which time she became violently sick and died in New York on January 30. Waite claimed that his mother-in-law knew she was dying and requested that she be cremated. Three months later, John Peck also visited his daughter, and he, too, died in New York.

A typical busy lunch hour at the Twentieth Century Café, circa 1940. Note the milkshake blenders on the counter. *Grand Rapids Public Library.*

Bowling centers also had lunch counters, and this one was in Northfield Lanes. *Grand Rapids Public Library.*

Waite planned to kill off all the family members until his wife was the sole heir. Then it would be Clara's turn! Arthur would have soon become a grieving widower, albeit a wealthy one, if an old family friend hadn't intervened. Fortunately, that friend contacted Clara's brother, Percy, to let him know that she was suspicious of Arthur Waite and feared for the rest of the Pecks. An ensuing autopsy revealed that John Peck had died of arsenic poisoning. It was assumed that his wife had, too. Waite realized that the gig was up and confessed to both murders. It turned out that his claim of being a physician proved false, and he had used the pretense to gain favor with Clara's family. He was brought to trial, found guilty and sentenced to death in the electric chair.

An ad in the July 7, 1948 edition of the *Grand Rapids Herald* showcased a casual alternative to hotel dining. The Red Hen Bar-B-Q specialized in barbecued chicken and ribs and was located at 317 Monroe Avenue between the Pantlind and Rowe Hotels. The Red Hen stayed open every day except

Sunday until 3:00 a.m., perfect for anyone downtown with a late-night case of the munchies. On Sundays, it closed at midnight. To further entice clientele, the 'cue was "prepared before your eyes on our Bar-B-Q machine in the window." And if barbecue wasn't what a customer craved, there were enough choices to tempt anyone's taste buds. Among numerous other options, customers could order an eighteen-ounce New York sirloin steak or, at the other end of the spectrum, waffles.

The Godwin Coffee Cup stayed in business only a little over ten years but made a lasting impression. There was nothing fancy about it, and it never pretended to be anything more than a coffee shop. In its earliest days, it would have been hard to spend much more than a dollar for lunch and not quite double that for dinner. The food was good and the surroundings plain, but the people, both the customers and the staff, were awesome. With so much competition, the owner, Henry Carpenter, spent his money on quality ingredients, not décor.

Peck's Drug Store on the south side of Campau Square was a popular lunch counter in the 1930s and needed counter stools, tables and booths to keep up with the demand. *Grand Rapids Public Museum.*

And it worked. These were people who worked hard and had lived through the Great Depression. They only cared about ambience when it was a special occasion, and on those rare occasions, they splurged and went somewhere else. Anyone dining on a supper of one pork chop, a potato, a vegetable, bread and butter, with coffee or tea included—and all for sixty cents—didn't expect candlelight and violins. The food tasted good, and someone else cooked it and washed the dishes. The Coffee Cup was just north of Thirty-sixth Street, it is remembered because it was a community gathering place. School kids went there for lunch, drawn in by Henry Carpenter's superior milkshakes.

In the end, it was simply one of those places that holds memories because life happened there. Ginnie Pratali remembered going there with her family at age six and losing a baby tooth in her hotdog. When she cried, the waitress saw that she was upset and gave her a scoop of ice cream. She had cried because two kids at another table laughed at her toothless grin.

CAFETERIAS

Cafeterias once enjoyed great popularity, and many could be found in downtown Grand Rapids. Some hotels had cafeterias in addition to their more upscale restaurants and offered a viable eat-and-run option to time-pressed guests. Hannaford's Cafeteria, in the Gilbert Building at the corner of Monroe Avenue and Commerce Street, served three meals daily. Although the earlier ones had tables decked in crisp white tablecloths, the service was simple. Diners progressed down the line, and after making their selections from the steam table's sizeable array, servers dished up the food.

The Fat Boy was another favorite and did so well downtown on Michigan Hill that the owner opened a second one on Plainfield Avenue. Both had the expected steam table staples of chicken, fish, ham, turkey, meatloaf (or another kind of beef) and liver and onions. Entrées rotated, with at least two choices each day. Throw in veggies, casseroles, coleslaw and premade salads that included a pineapple ring and cottage cheese on a lettuce leaf. Along with slices of pie and cake, there was usually red or green Jell-O topped with a dollop of whipped cream and a choice of chocolate or tapioca pudding.

At least one cafeteria owner believed that men should have the option of dining in cafeterias without being troubled by the presence of women, a presumption that would be laughed at today. The *Grand Rapids Spectator*, published by the chamber of commerce forerunner, the Association of

When this downtown Fat Boy Cafeteria did even better than expected, the owner opened a second one on Plainfield Avenue. *Grand Rapids Public Library.*

Commerce, ran an ad in 1927 for the Chinnick's various enterprises. The company owned the Stag Cafeteria for men, located at 119 Pearl Street, and also offered bowling and a barbershop. Chinnick's other businesses were the Family Cafeteria at 41 Ionia Avenue and a billiard parlor at 91 Monroe Avenue. There were stag bars at the time, and private men's clubs were the norm. But a men-only cafeteria? Makes you wonder what they were doing in there.

The company also owned Chinnick's Michigan Room, a fine dining establishment, at a time when a porterhouse steak could be had for $1.35, a martini for $0.35 and beers starting at $0.10. It would be a nickel more if you wanted your brew in a bottle.

The YWCA operated a cafeteria for its residents that was also open to the public at bargain prices, a courtesy much appreciated by downtown

Above: Even young ladies who resided elsewhere sometimes dined at the YWCA. It was a good meeting spot for these three members of the Martha League. *Grand Rapids Public Library.*

Opposite: Cafeterias like Schensul's fell victim to all-you-can-eat buffets. *Author's collection.*

officeworkers with limited amounts of both time and money. Even if they weren't lodging there, the cafeteria provided a non-threatening spot for young ladies to dine.

Schensul's had two cafeterias in Grand Rapids, one on Twenty-eighth Street in the Rogers Plaza shopping mall and the other near the Interstate 96 and U.S. Highway 131 on Plainfield Avenue. The one at Rogers Plaza did especially well, as it drew in workers in the area as well as mall shoppers. In its heyday, Rogers Plaza (the first enclosed mall in southwest Michigan) was anchored by Montgomery Ward at one end and Turnstyle at the other. In between were popular shops of the day, including Gantos' and Beverley's, both of which specialized in women's clothing and accessories.

Cafeterias in general lost favor with the fickle public, and both Schensul's spots were gone by about 1980. Except for hospitals and schools, few cafeterias are around today. America's supersize-me mentality spawned the

Schensul's **"America's Finest Cafeterias"**

KALAMAZOO - S. MALL

GRAND RAPIDS - ROGERS PLAZA

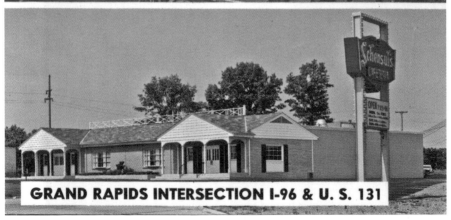

GRAND RAPIDS INTERSECTION I-96 & U. S. 131

all-you-can-eat eateries like the Golden Corral or the Old Country Buffet. Unlike the cafeterias, which served standard portions, the new buffets are the kind of place where filling one's plate more than once can seem as much of a responsibility as a challenge.

CHAPTER 5

A Pinch of This and a Dash of That

The country club life was and still is for the privileged among us. That said, those with the means—and, in too many cases, the pedigree—to join could count on gracious dining along with golf, tennis and all the other amenities.

Grand Rapids' Kent Country Club has had a long and fabled history since 1901. Josephine Bender, whose family had long been associated with the club, wrote about its history in a booklet, *When Kent Was Young: An Early History and Reminiscence*. She waxed poetic on the talents of longtime chef Ida Jarreo, stating, "Ida's reputation for mouth-watering menus became widespread. No one treated to her cold planked trout, masked in its delectable sauce, her delicious small rolls or her famous French dressing (she would never reveal the recipe) was apt to forget them."

One thing that would not be tolerated today was that women did not have full membership. Wives, daughters and other ladies gained admittance only through a male member. Interestingly, that chauvinist policy did not extend to the kitchen. Wives were often called on to help with preparations for special events. It was noted that Mrs. John Blodgett Sr. provided soft-shell crabs for a luncheon in honor of a visiting dignitary. Instead of cooking, Mrs. Blodgett should have been cooked for, as she was a pillar of local society in her own right, as well as the wife of one of the city's most prominent men, the person for whom Blodgett Hospital was named.

In 1985, *Grand Rapids* magazine introduced the "Rapids," the city's very own drink. It was created to honor the diverse ethnic groups of Grand

Rapids' past. Ingredients paid homage to the area's rich ethnic diversity. Perrier water represented the rapids on which the city was founded, as well as the French fur traders. Vodka was a nod to the Polish immigrants, and Vandermint Dutch Chocolate Liqueur celebrated the contributions of the Dutch settlers.

It was served in many of the local restaurants, including Grootmoeders Tafel and Cygnus, both in the Amway Grand Plaza. Soon, variations started popping up: the "Grand Rapids" was a double, and the non-alcoholic "Calm Rapids" replaced the Vandermint with Hershey's syrup and peppermint extract and omitted the vodka.

The late 1970s and early 1980s brought a new style of dining to the city. As the allure of the hippie lifestyle faded, yuppies ascended. Some might think of money as dirty, but it's still the currency required in modern-day life. The prevailing attitude became that if you're going to have to work anyway, you might as well earn enough to live well. It wasn't long before three-piece suits outnumbered tie-dyed tees and Birkenstocks.

Those career-oriented young professionals and wannabes demanded sophisticated dining options mixed with casual ambience. They chose wine and cheese over beer and pretzels. "Bars" became "lounges" with hanging ferns and stained glass where people could unwind, talk business and, later, when the music started, boogie. Responsible lounge owners offered happy-hour munchies in the hopes of reducing the effects of the alcohol. Many gave free non-alcoholic beverages to a group's designated driver.

Yuppies gathered in the lounges of the new chain steakhouses like the Cork and Cleaver, Mountain Jack's and the Stag and Hound. Another British offering, in name and in theme, was the Knightsbridge Inn. Menu choices at the Inn had contrived names, such as the house specialties the Knight's Feast or the King's Feast. Diners could choose entrées under several headings, including Ye Olde Round Table Choices, the Knight's Delight, Sir Lancelot's Choice and the Provident Crusader. For the smaller appetite, there was a section called Guinevere's Selection. True Anglophiles immediately noticed that it failed to list anything even remotely British. No ye olde Yorkshire pudding. No bubble and squeak. Even a pseudo-British eatery ought to be able to dish up some sticky toffee pudding. Scones with clotted cream, anyone?

It was the era that ushered in TGI Friday's, although Friday was celebrated as singles' night out, not the end of the workweek. Don't forget that these were people for whom nothing was as important as their careers. All but the Friday's are long gone, but they have been replaced by newer chains like the Outback and Logan's, thus forcing more beloved local establishments to close for good. Somewhere along the way, America has become a homogenized society with no room for the local character that once distinguished one city from another. On the plus side, today's dining and watering holes are smoke-free, so a night out no longer means a trip to the dry cleaner to remove the smell of stale cigarette smoke.

Most people wouldn't think of combining Wurlitzer theater organs and pizza, but the Roaring Twenties Pizza did exactly that and did it beautifully. One of two organists, Charlie Balogh or Donna Parker, gave two performances daily and wore festive red velvet adorned with gold braids. The Mighty Wurlitzer theater pipe organ previously had a fifteen-year run providing music and other sound effects for silent movies. When talking movies rendered it obsolete, it was placed in storage by a private owner until the new owners of the Roaring Twenties gave it renewed life. With multiple pedals, keyboards and more than two thousand pipes ranging in size from sixteen inches in diameter to about the size of a pencil, it was a commanding presence.

The food was good, but the big draw was the entertainment. Along with pizza, the menu offered sandwiches and other Italian fare. For a few years, it was great fun to nosh on pizza and then enjoy a singalong. A manager from the now-closed Reynolds Metals Company extrusion plant on Porter Street at Burlingame Avenue enjoyed taking business visitors there as a refreshing change from the usual night on the town of drinks and upscale dining.

Another short-lived entertainment venue, the Stagetrunk Dinner Theater, brought diners and theatergoers to Plainfield Avenue in the 1970s and put on a full range of musical, comedic and dramatic productions. Food was buffet-style. It isn't known exactly why it was closed when such enterprises thrived in other cities.

The Russo Family

The Russo name has a long and storied Grand Rapids history, and in one way or another, it all revolved around food. Ranging from groceries to a banquet hall to a nightclub to the pizzerias, the family of G.B. Russo has seen it all. It all began with G.B.'s grocery store on South Division Avenue. The family lived above the store, a common practice among European immigrants who owned businesses, as the line between family and work was often indistinct. A fire that started next to their building quickly burned out of control and damaged their home and business. The Russo building was not insured, but the family was able to repair the damages and reopen the grocery.

The renovation spawned another idea. G.B. remodeled some of the second floor and turned it into a hall that he would rent out for special events. He believed that a sizeable portion of his business would be Italian weddings. He named it Roma Hall, which immediately set it apart from the multitude of Polish halls, and opened for business sometime in 1930. It was not the best time to start that kind of business, as Prohibition had not yet ended and the country was still suffering through the Great Depression.

The funny thing about ideas is that one leads to another and then another. G.B. was on a roll, and for a time he decided against renting out Roma Hall on a regular basis, instead preferring to have his own nightclub in the space. He called it the Genoa Café and featured floor shows, food, drink and dance bands. The food was Italian and the crowd appreciative. An old ad notes that the spaghetti dinner was fifty cents, and the club also served ravioli and chicken. The floor show featured Erna Clark, a torch singer, and a tap dancer named Pat LaRue. Curiously, it listed the dance band as the Royal Victorians Orchestra and billed it as "the fastest dance band in West Michigan." Who knew that dancing was a speed sport? Although the food was Italian, the beer was Old Dutch.

On the days the club was closed, he rented Roma Hall for private parties, political rallies, conventions, public dances and the black cotillion debutante balls. His children all became involved in the various enterprises, and the Russo family became a force to be reckoned with.

Roma Hall was expanded, enlarging the space by more than one-third, allowing the family to host two events simultaneously. The Genoa Café, renamed the Russo Café after its first year, closed, but Russo's Pizzeria had been opened next to the grocery store and was still going strong. By the late 1930s, and continuing until the early 1980s, the Grand Rapids African American community rented the hall on a regular basis and brought in Muddy Waters and B.B. King, among other nationally known performers, on a list that grew to include the Supremes, who were then in the early days of their career and known as the Primettes. They were in Roma Hall to open for Mary Wells. G.B.'s nephew, Frank Russo, was working in the pizzeria when the group stopped in for supper after the show. Almost anyone who was anyone in doo-wop, blues or gospel at one time or another graced the Roma Hall stage.

Soon, a group of the city's black businessmen decided that another performance hall was in order and organized the Indigo Club. No, the Russos didn't manage it or even supply the food. But they owned the building, which was located just down Division Avenue from the Roma Hall, and once again were in the role of renting hall space. Sadly, after a little more than five decades, the building housing Roma Hall was deemed unsafe and demolished.

That still wasn't the end of the Russo family's contribution to Grand Rapids dining. G.B.'s brother, Joe, carried on the tradition. Joe's many talents could have led to show business, as he was a drummer and had played in some local bands. For a time, he had a friend in the White House, having played on the South High School football team with Jerry Ford. Joe's entry into the restaurant business was a nightclub named Indian Village. It was located in Wyoming in the 3800 block of South Division Avenue, near Bigelow Field. His grandmother, Jennie, cooked the Italian cuisine at the Indian Village, and her food was one of the draws.

Genoa Café, Russo's Café, Roma Hall, Indigo Club and the Indian Village are all gone. Russo's retail store remains, though in a new location, and specializes in imported and specialty items. The cheeses are the best around, and the gelato is rich and creamy, exactly the way it should be. There are still two Russo's Pizza Shops.

Some claim that the Russo family had the first pizzeria in southwest Michigan, but that is incorrect. Fricano's Pizza Tavern in Grand Haven was the first. The Russo Pizzeria on Division Avenue may have been the first in Grand Rapids, and it's certain that G.B. served the first pizza, but it was in the Roma Hall.

Anyone with a sweet tooth who grew up in the Burton Heights neighborhood will remember Sweetland's, a Division Avenue icon for seventeen years before moving to Plainfield Avenue. Using only the freshest of choice ingredients, the Naum family produced some of the best palate-pleasing treats to be found. They made ice cream daily, and fountain confections included old-fashioned sodas, malts and sundaes. Another popular item was a sinfully rich mud pie consisting of a rich chocolate cookie crust and coffee ice cream crowned with freshly whipped cream and milk chocolate hot fudge sauce.

In the unlikely event that this didn't produce enough of a sugar high, the shop also specialized in hand-dipped chocolates made from the recipes of three generations of Naums. Sweetland's definitely knew how to market, and it displayed those mouthwatering confections in glass cases near the cash register. Even customers completely sated after an ice cream dessert were tempted to take chocolates home—individually or by boxes ranging from one to five pounds. Yum! Sweetland's is still going strong with three area retail stores and is owned and operated by another generation of Naums.

CHAPTER 6
Diners and Drive-Ins

*E*ven more colorful than the neighborhood hole-in-the-wall cafés themselves were the regulars who frequented them. Terry's Sandwich Shop on Burton Street in Wyoming's Galewood neighborhood had at least one of those characters. It also had a steep step just inside the door. Carolyn Lucas was running late for a lunch date with friends when she charged in and forgot to step up. Next thing she knew, she was sprawled on the floor and feeling lucky that nothing but her pride was injured. Before she could get up, an elderly gentleman who had been seated at the counter dashed to her aid. He helped her to her feet and then steered her to the booth where her friends sat giggling over the spectacle she had made of herself. "I had to help her, the antique little thing," her rescuer explained. Those giggles exploded into hoots.

"I was all of thirty-five, so I can only hope he meant to say 'petite,'" Lucas explained. Every time she went back to Terry's, he was holding down the same stool at the counter, where he apparently held court on a regular basis, ever ready to help the next klutzy damsel in distress.

BURGERS IN THE CITY

It's hard to believe, but once upon a time burger joints were individual establishments, each with its own character. They weren't lined up like peas in a pod on franchise row, as there were no franchise rows. Each neighborhood had its own, sometimes more than one, and the owners didn't need enormous television advertising budgets to draw clientele. All they needed was an occasional newspaper ad and word of mouth.

Ritzee's Hamburg Shop was the most eye-popping of the local burger palaces and was intentionally built to stand out among the competition. One thing that made the otherwise typical one-story diner-type eatery stand out was the bright green-and-yellow painted exterior, but mostly it was the two-and-a-half-story tower on the front. About two-thirds up the tower, in a circle, was the Ritzee logo, a formally dressed gentleman holding a cane and tipping his top hat. "Ritzee's Hamburgs" was printed inside the circle, along with the slogan, "The snack that makes you come back."

Inside was the expected counter with stools, as well as a few tables. Ritzee's also offered curb service and could accommodate about sixty cars. It opened in 1940, way back when a burger cost a dime, and it was located at 6 East Park Place, near Park Church, then called Park Congregational Church. Business was brisk for a period of about ten and a half years. It was razed when it became obvious that a single-story structure, not counting the

Ritzee's Hamburgs might not have been the only burger palace downtown, but it was the most eye-popping. *Grand Rapids Public Library.*

decorative tower, with a sixty-car parking lot was not the best use of prime real estate in a rapidly growing city.

Another gone-but-not-forgotten downtown favorite was Bono's Burger House. When Russ and Leona Bono shuttered their shop in 1973, they said that their Division Avenue and Crescent Street eatery had first "fed the guys that built downtown, and then fed the guys that tore it down so they could build it again." That referred to the massive rebuilding projects in downtown Grand Rapids in the 1970s.

By the 1950s and '60s, hamburgers had become the sandwich of first choice for so many Americans that chains, both local and national, sprung up like dandelions after a good rain, for the primary purpose of flipping ground beef patties to meet the ever-growing demand.

FABLES

The last three of the fabled Fables Restaurants closed in 2000 and are still sorely missed. Fables Restaurant's perfectly battered and deep-fried onion rings became the gold standard, and no other place has filled the void. Burger lovers had their favorite, and the top choices were the DeLuxe Beefburg; the Mr. Fabulous burger, which lived up to its name; and the Oliveburger. Service was cafeteria style, and it was the first in the area to serve English muffin bread.

The local chain began in 1953, when cousins Richard (Dick) Faber and John Boyles took over the Kewpee Burger stand from John's father, Gerald. They played with the letters in Faber and Boyle and came up Fables. Dick was the detail man and had been known to retrain kitchen workers he didn't think were putting enough lettuce on the sandwiches. He made it a point to visit restaurants when they were closed to make clandestine cleanliness inspections. It was not merely scribbled notes on things he wanted done—he lugged around an old clunky portable typewriter and left detailed instructions.

That kind of hands-on attention guaranteed success, and the chain grew to seventeen restaurants. The cousins then partnered with Dan Wallace and founded Savory Street. They sold Fables, along with their secret recipes, in 1988. Unfortunately, the new owners thought that no one would notice if they cut a corner here or there. When it affected quality, people did notice. Longtime customers abandoned the chain when products no longer lived up to their expectations. One by one, the restaurants closed.

George Buris had already established a reputation in Muskegon for operating one of the best barbecue restaurants in west Michigan when he brought George Buris Famous Barbecue to 697 Twenty-eighth Street in Wyoming, east of Highway 131. Dick Bolema managed the local facility and offered taste-tempting pork, beef and ham flavored with secret sauces and slow-cooked on rotisseries over a gas flame in a detached brick shed.

Noted for complete dinners as well as mouthwatering sandwiches, the eatery was open every day except Sunday from eleven o'clock in the morning until midnight. Buris's barbecue proved as successful in Grand Rapids as it had been in Muskegon, and eight years after opening, he sold the business. The menu remained basically unchanged, although the name changed to the Torch.

The restaurant changed hands again, and new owner Dean Loomis removed the barbecue shed, came up with a whole new menu and renamed it Dean's 24-Hour Café. Dean kept it going another fifteen years. In its latest incarnation, it is going strong as the Golden 28 Chinese, Vietnamese and Korean Restaurant.

It's no surprise that the Godwin Heights area on South Division Avenue became a hotbed of restaurants, taverns and drive-ins. Division Avenue is a main street, and Godwin Heights is a neighborhood in the Wyoming industrial area that began when General Motors opened a stamping plant on Thirty-sixth Street. Other large manufacturers soon followed suit. Reynolds Metals Company built an extrusion plant originally called Extruded Metals to produce aluminum needs for World War II. Another General Motors plant followed. There was Kelvinator and Lear Siegler. Wyoming experienced phenomenal growth as retail outlets and providers of services joined the exodus from the city. New schools were built and existing ones enlarged. Housing boomed. New neighborhoods sprung up like spring daffodils as people flocked to the area to be closer to their jobs and also to enjoy a pleasant suburban lifestyle. That pleasant lifestyle definitely included restaurants of all kinds.

Drive-ins, especially, were plentiful and included Candy Ann's, owned by Bob and Evelyn Christensen and named for their firstborn child. Candy Ann herself posed for the sign, and the photographer is said to have had a difficult time completing the image before she ate the burger in her hand. The couple opened a second restaurant, Scottie's, on Twenty-eighth Street when their second child came along.

Candy Ann's was on the corner of South Division Avenue and Fiftieth Street in Kelloggsville. When drive-ins fell out of favor, the Christensens converted Candy Ann's into a full-service restaurant called the Edge.

Most burger places offered curb service, where a toot of the horn brought a carhop, often on roller skates, to take your order. For teens, the food was never the draw. It was all about being there, being seen and seeing who was with whom. It was that last part that Patsy Gaulding and Carole Williams remembered most.

Patsy had a brand-new driver's license and drove her mom's car to celebrate with her best friend, Carole. Their two-chicks-in-a-Chevy-Bel-Aire-night-on-the-town started with the obligatory stop at Candy Ann's. From there it turned ugly. Patsy spotted a familiar Ford and realized that her steady boyfriend, a young man who shall remain nameless, was there with another girl. The way the two were necking, it became instantly obvious that Mr. Nameless wasn't going quite as steady as Patsy. For those not schooled in the social lingo of the time, "necking" was what couples indulged in at neck level and above. Any lower groping was called "petting." So-called good girls had occasionally been known to pet, but never, ever at a drive-in restaurant. When it came to drive-in movies, however, all bets were off.

Patsy did what any late 1950s/early 1960s girl would do in similar circumstances. She demanded an immediate strategy meeting in the ladies' room. That was the first mistake. After exploring their limited options, they decided it best to order a burger and a shake, eat fast, act nonchalant and get the heck out of Dodge. Plan complete, they tried opening the restroom door, but the doorknob came off in Carole's hand. After what seemed an eternity, but was probably no more than five minutes, someone came to the door and then went to fetch the manager. Cheers erupted from those sitting inside when the two red-faced girls were rescued.

In her haste, Patsy had locked the car with the key still in the ignition. That was the second mistake and meant going back inside to the manager, who already thought they were idiots, and confirming his opinion by asking to use his phone. Patsy's dad came with the spare key, as well as a lecture he delivered in front of anyone in hearing distance. Her only consolation was that Mr. Nameless and his babe du jour had long since departed. Other school acquaintances remained, however, and she could see them laughing in the background.

"I spent the whole night wondering how I could convince Mom and Dad to let me change schools," she said. In one of the many postmortems held on the following day, the two realized that the whole humiliation need never have happened. They were in the car by themselves, so why had they felt the need to talk in the ladies' room? Patsy said that her German grandmother would have had the perfect answer: "Too soon old, and too late smart."

At 2907 South Division was the Root Beer Barrel, popular with Godwin Heights High School students during the week and the area at large on weekends. It opened in the 1940s, built by Paul and Della Wicks. First called the B&K, a manager came up with the more descriptive name shortly after opening. It was another of a surfeit of drive-ins and was closed in the mid-'50s when a used car shop moved into the space.

Wimpy's, located in a Pullman diner, was the hands-down favorite in the Godwin Heights area and a hangout for Godwin High School students. While all the food was good, the local hotspot was known especially for its burgers and chili dogs. The unoriginal name was no doubt inspired by the perennial button-popping, burger-chomping character of *Popeye* comic strip fame. This was during the time when every city in America had a drive-in named Wimpy's.

A.J. Potter started this Wimpy's in 1935, and in addition to curb service, there were ten stools at the counter. The carhops were all boys, and most were Godwin Heights High School students. A.J. brought the first foot-long hot dogs to the area and had to have extra-long buns specially made. The restaurant introduced its new frosty malts in various flavors to great reviews, and all seemed well.

Before colas became most people's soft drink of first choice, root beer reigned, and stands like this one on Division Avenue in Wyoming were everywhere. Some were even shaped like root beer barrels. *Wyoming Historical Commission.*

Wimpy's success was, in part, attributed to being the first area drive-in to offer foot-long hotdogs. It is tucked away here, but in its heyday it was the hands-down favorite. *Grand Rapids Public Library.*

Then Wimpy's was forced to move the diner over a land issue. The new location was only nine blocks north on Division to the 3100 block, across from the Southlawn Theater. That short a distance should not have made any difference, but it did, and Wimpy's never regained its momentum. It transformed itself into the Wimpy's Chickee Drive-in. The chili, hotdogs and malts remained on the menu, but as the name implied, the new emphasis was on fried chicken. It was short-lived, as by then fast-food chains had crowded out most of the locally owned and operated mom and pop operations. Kentucky Fried Chicken had a bigger advertising budget and was able to convince people that its chicken was better.

The weekly suburban newspaper ran a piece about the Octagon Restaurant at 4428 Division Avenue and called it "the Sanitary Eating Place in the Home Acres neighborhood." There was no indication of why it was singled out or if there was any reason to believe the competition was unsanitary. At that time, Bob Gilman was the owner, and maybe he adopted the slogan to set himself apart, although most restaurants claim to have the best food and expect the public to assume it is prepared in a clean kitchen.

Swayne's Bar-B-Q was the place to go when it celebrated its grand opening, especially if you were a child. The restaurant advertised free malts to all kids that day, and the response was overwhelming. During the busiest part of the day, the creamy confections had to be served in the parking lot, as the crowd far exceeded the interior capacity. The event was a huge success, and those free malts ended up buying a lot of customer loyalty. Many people still remember waiting for their turn and how good the malt tasted when it finally came.

It didn't take as much to make us happy in those simpler times. How many of the kids shown in that crowd chose to go to Swayne's after Little League games, music lessons and, later, with their dates after a movie at the nearby Studio 28? And those free malts were the reason why.

Drive-ins seemed to be in competition over who could come up with the catchiest name. In Wee Go, Here T'is, Dopey's and Kum Bak were

Swayne's Bar-B-Q celebrated its grand opening with free malts for all children. *Grand Rapids Public Library.*

So many children came to Swayne's Bar-B-Q's grand opening that it had to take the party outside to the parking lot. *Grand Rapids Public Library.*

a few of suburban Wyoming's examples. The Kum Bak opened at 1105 Twenty-eighth Street, SW, in September 1959 and was managed by Secret and Marianne Ybema, who lived in the immediate neighborhood at 918 Buckingham Avenue. That was another good thing about living and working in Wyoming. Sometimes the commute could be done on foot.

In Wee Go was eventually taken over by Kewpee, becoming the third outlet of that small local burger shop, and owned by Gerald Boyles. The location, on Twenty-eighth Street opposite the Beltline Theater, was golden and was worth the expense of renovations. After upgrading all the equipment and hiring new management, it reopened with better traffic flow that made for faster service.

One of the more interesting buildings to house a diner on Division Avenue was an old trolley car. When Grand Rapids replaced trolleys with buses, the old cars were repurposed into everything from hunting cabins to chicken coops and restaurants. This particular trolley car changed hands numerous times between the late 1930s and the 1950s. It isn't known what it was called in its first incarnations, but through most of the 1940s it was the popular Five-Star Grill. Then it became Baker's Lunch and, finally, Hogan's Diner. That is quite a history for a trolley car that the first owner bought for a dollar.

In an odd twist of fate, General Motors, the very company responsible for the start of so many local businesses, put at least one restaurant out of business. Because it was touted as the company that yanked Grand Rapids out of the Depression, it came as no surprise that whatever GM wanted, GM got. What it wanted was for Birchwood Avenue to stop before it reached Thirty-sixth Street.

Unfortunately for Leta Louks, who had opened Smittie's Little Jem on the corner of Birchwood and Thirty-sixth, that corner would no longer exist, and that spelled the end of Smittie's Little Jem.

Not all the restaurants were drive-ins. The Log Cabin Bar-B-Q on Division Avenue, a little north of Twenty-eighth Street, started out as a sit-down eatery and served a lot more than barbecued ribs. It's still around, although the restaurant part is gone. Somewhere along the way, it transformed itself into a drinking establishment complete with karaoke and beer pong.

The In Wee Go staff has all the bases covered at this popular drive-in that was eventually acquired by the Kewpee restaurant company. *Grand Rapids Public Library.*

Kids of all ages found it fun to eat at the Kewpee Drive-in. *Grand Rapids Public Library.*

The Log Cabin, once a popular restaurant, still exists, but only as a bar. *Wyoming Historical Commission.*

The Casa Via at 4560 South Division Avenue was one of a handful of motels in the area when owner Ronald Eyer upped its appeal by adding a full-service restaurant to the property. Jessie Wright and Don Lowe were the first to manage it. Don brought with him experience as an army mess hall sergeant followed by several years of working in "restaurants of high repute" in Grand Rapids and Phoenix, Arizona. The duo served up full steak and chicken dinners along with short-order choices. Jack Sullivan was the next chef, and he increased business by staying open longer hours.

Even with the abundance of eating choices on Division, the Casa Via captured the market of those looking for a place to eat, crash and then eat again before dashing off to their final destination. The restaurant, also called Casa Via, disappeared completely, but the motel lives on as an efficiency apartment building.

I SCREAM, YOU SCREAM, WE ALL SCREAM FOR ICE CREAM

Many Grand Rapids residents have fond memories of Farrell's Ice Cream Parlor on Twenty-eighth Street at Woodland Mall. It had enough gimmicks to make it good fun and was often the site of birthday parties and other celebrations.

One favorite choice was the Disaster, brought to the table on a stretcher and accompanied by a wailing siren. And who could forget the Pig Trough, containing, among other ingredients, one scoop each of every available flavor? Anyone devouring the whole thing was serenaded with a rousing rendition of "[Fill-in-the-blank] made a pig of himself/herself at Farrell's."

As guests left, they were given a chance to receive a free rope of licorice. All they had to do was recite perfectly, "Farrell's features fabulous food and fantastic fountain fantasies for frolicking fun-filled festive families." Try saying that with an ice cream induced brain freeze.

Other much-loved ice cream shops from the past were Miller's Dairy and Buth's Dairy. Among perennial favorites are Jersey Junction in East Grand Rapids' Gaslight Village on Twenty-eighth Street and anywhere that serves Hudsonville ice cream, now made in nearby Holland but which originated in the farm area of Hudsonville.

Rosie's Diner

Remember that old television commercial where Nancy Walker played a no-nonsense diner operator who relied on "the quicker-picker-upper" Bounty paper towels? It was filmed at Rosie's Diner. At that time, Rosie's was located in Flint, Michigan. In 1987, Jerry Berta bought the restaurant and moved it to the Grand Rapids suburb of Rockford. But he didn't serve food until 1991, and even then only because he was forced into it. He had bought the diner to use as an art gallery. Both he and his wife, Madeline, are artists, and it seemed like an economical venue in which to show and sell their work. The people who stopped, however, only wanted to buy burgers and shakes. He finally installed a neon sign that read, "No Food, Just Art." Even that failed to stop hungry folks seeking diner food in what certainly looked like a diner. If it walks like a duck and it quacks like a duck…

It was time to execute Plan B. Jerry went into the food business by buying a second diner, this one from Ralph Corrado, who had renamed his dad's Farmland Diner Rosie's after the old TV ad. In its early days, it had been patronized by a New Jersey kid named Frank who loved to sing. The kid's last name was Sinatra. Jerry had Rosie's transported from Little Ferry, New

Rosie's Diner closed in 2011 and stands unoccupied. *Norma Lewis.*

Jersey. That sounds easier than it turned out to be. The seven-hundred-mile trip to Rockford took four days, the reasons being a fire and ten flat tires.

In spite of that, he was by then hooked on diners. His next project for the property he then called Dinerland was to have been an eighteen-hole diner-themed miniature golf course. That never quite got off the ground, but he did acquire another diner. This one was from New York, and it was to be another restaurant serving a different style cuisine. That plan failed, and the newest diner ended up as a seldom-used banquet and special events venue.

Rosie's Diner was a success, though. Jerry had planned to hire someone else to operate the diner, but nobody wanted the job so he ended up doing it himself. With no advertising other than a sign and word of mouth, opening day crowds lined up outside the door. Paper towels were not the Rockford Rosie's only claim to fame; it was also once featured on the *Diners, Drive-Ins and Dives* TV show.

The food was good, and he had a great staff and loyal customers. For a while, Jerry had fun operating the place, but eventually he wanted to go back to his first love: art. He had hoped to sell Rosie's but was unable to find a buyer. He remained in business, reluctantly, until 2011. At that time, there was a fourth diner on the premises that had not yet been put to use. That's when Jerry Berta got out of the food service business permanently so that he could concentrate on his artistic endeavors full time. But Rosie had made her mark to the point that the Madame Alexander doll company even introduced a Rosie the Waitress doll.

CHAPTER 7

Historic Treasures Still Going Strong

CHERIE INN

The Cherie Inn is found at 969 Cherry Street in the East Hills business district where Diamond, Wealthy and Lake Drive come together and has been a local institution since 1924. Although the Art Deco exterior appears a tad lackluster, a new sign featuring the Eiffel Tower hints at the subdued elegance contained within. It never disappoints. Add a sidewalk café area and this place could indeed be in Paris.

The furnishings are Grand Rapids–made, 1940s-vintage Stickley. The tin on the ceiling is original to the building. Fresh flowers adorn each table, and plants flourish on the sunny windowsills. Because the space is divided into three separate dining areas, it can accommodate large groups while still providing a quiet space for a small party, a romantic duo or someone simply wishing to read a newspaper while sipping coffee and dining alone.

Open only for breakfast and lunch, it's a place that delivers on its promise of an exceptional meal in a serene setting. Cherie claims to serve the best eggs Benedict in town, and anyone who has tasted them would be hard-pressed to disagree. Thin-sliced ham replaces the more commonplace Canadian bacon, and the rich, creamy hollandaise sauce is to die for. Add the restaurant's version of a mimosa (pomegranate juice, pineapple juice and Sprite) and it is heaven.

According to Kay O'Hallaran, that hollandaise sauce is her only problem. "The first time I went there, I had eggs Benedict. It was so good I've never

Cherie Inn, in the East Hills neighborhood, continues its long tradition of understated elegance. *Grand Rapids Public Library.*

been able to make myself order anything else." Sometimes she wonders what she may be missing, but as soon as she tucks into those eggs, she is pretty sure she has not missed a thing.

Michael Kulczyk has owned the Cherie Inn since 1997 and makes certain that guests still receive the seamless service and exceptional menu that have defined the restaurant for more than ninety years.

THE BELTLINE BAR: HOME OF THE WET BURRITO

Jeff Lobdell has been in the Grand Rapids–area restaurant business a relatively short time, only since 2002, but during those years he has made a name for himself in the industry. His company, Restaurant Partners Inc., owns ten area restaurants. Others are Grand Coney, Sundance, Bagel Beanery, Omelette Shoppe, Forest Hills Inn, Flap Jack Shack, Prime Time Pub, BLT and El Barrio. He specializes in buying properties from retiring owners. Lobdell has served as president of the Michigan Restaurant Association and is active in the national organization. Once, when lobbying in Washington on issues concerning his industry, he packed and shipped Beltline Bar's famous wet burritos to Michigan's Second District congressman, Bill Huizenga, and his staff in celebration of Cinco de Mayo.

If Jeff sounds like an overachiever, he can't help it. It's a family trait. His father, Wayne, grew up in poverty and overcame seemingly insurmountable odds to become an entrepreneur, also in the restaurant business. Among his varied business ventures were several Kentucky Fried Chicken franchises. In his memoir, *Climb from the Cellar*, Wayne Lobdell credited his father, Howard, with instilling in him a strong work ethic. Whenever he was hired to do any odd jobs in the neighborhood, Howard always told him to do more than the job for which he was hired. The advice served him well, and he passed it on to his sons.

As for that wet burrito, it is the result of a mistake, and that mistake made the Beltline famous. When former owner Jerry Rutkowski was on vacation, his supplier delivered oversized soft shells. Lunchtime was growing close, so the chef had to think of a creative way to use those shells. He rose to the challenge and made a variation of the usual burrito and then experimented with seasonings for the perfect sauce. A short time later, the lunch crowd started pouring in. The chef introduced his creation, a new Tex-Mex dish called (drum roll, please) the wet burrito. A legend was born. The wet burrito put the Beltline on the map, and Jerry's patrons made him keep it on the menu.

Rumor has it that pregnant women have found the wet burrito a reliable labor inducer when Mother Nature drags her feet. That's subjective, though, and the author's daughter swears by the ribs at Z's downtown on Campau Promenade. Whatever the reason for ordering the burritos, and as good as they are, there are many more reasons to visit the Beltline. Some of the best are the ground beef enchiladas and the sizzling fajitas. Try the homemade guacamole—it's a safe bet that you'll never buy guacamole in the dairy aisle again. If you think the only Mexican desserts are those not-quite-sweet-

Beltline Bar owner Jeff Lobdell with three of his longtime employees. Beside Jeff is Cindie Levett. On the left are Chris Ackerman and Cherish Ellen. Their combined years of employment equal eighty-one, with Jeff and Cindie the new kids on the block with only fourteen years each. On the table in front of Jeff is the signature wet burrito. *Shelby Ayers.*

enough cookies found in most places, treat yourself to an apple burrito or chimi cheesecake. Don't forget the margaritas.

Jeff believes that the Beltline is successful for a number of reasons. First is the quality of the food. He never cuts corners and believes in buying locally. He always buys from the same butcher and has never bought grated cheese, in spite of the inconvenience of grating it in-house. Then there is the secret spice recipe that Jerry gave him.

He also gives credit to his staff. Many employees have been there for decades, and there have been times when two generations of a family have worked there at the same time. They are loyal, and Jeff greatly appreciates that loyalty. One employee took that loyalty a bit too far, however, and the result could have been deadly. An older lady, close to retirement, was working as hostess one night and must have looked like an easy mark to the man who came in by himself. He told her that he had a gun and demanded money. She calmly pushed an emergency call button to summon police. That was followed by an impolite phrase that let him know for certain that no money would be changing hands on her watch. Then she told him to get out. He did, but not quite fast enough, as the police caught him a short distance away.

NICK FINK'S

Nick Fink's in Comstock Park is a few blocks south of Fifth/Third Field, home of the Detroit Tigers' farm team, the Grand Rapids Whitecaps. In 1888, Nick Fink, a Prussian immigrant, opened what was originally called the Riversite Hotel at what is now 3965 West River in Comstock Park. It remains open today and is the oldest continually operating tavern in the Grand Rapids area. It has been a hotel, a tavern, a post office, a barbershop and a brothel. He passed it down to Nicks II, III and IV.

Nick II made local history in 1905 when he accomplished the first recorded flight in Kent County. Using a bicycle to which he had attached wings resembling a box kite, he soared off the tavern roof. His flight ended abruptly (and painfully) when he crashed into a telegraph pole and fractured his collarbone.

Ernest Hemingway made a point of stopping there while traveling from Oak Park, Illinois, to his family's summer home on Walloon Lake, near Petoskey, Michigan. He is said to have based some of the characters in his Nick Adams stories on men he met at Nick Fink's. Best of all, it still looks like the kind of place where "Papa" would enjoy holding down a barstool.

The restaurant fell on hard times when ownership left the Fink family but has been revitalized since being purchased by the Gilmore Group, the same company that owns Mangiamo!, now located in the former Gibson's Restaurant. The folks at Gilmore have a talent for taking on old buildings and creating something new and special. At Fink's, they did an admirable job of refurbishing while hanging on to the original character.

The years have brought many changes. Customers no longer drop in after a day at the nearby Grand River Speedrome racetrack, as it closed in 1966. The West Michigan Fairgrounds closed even earlier, in 1937. Today, patrons might stop by for a cool one after attending a Whitecaps game. Locals make up a large part of the customer base.

On the company website, the tavern uses wordplay to announce that Fink's has the most reasonably priced drinks in the area and claims that they definitely lift spirits. However, that means more than spirits in drinks, as the place is said to be haunted. Manager and chef Matt Rule admitted that strange things really do happen. On three separate occasions, ghost hunters have reported paranormal activity. Not to worry. The ghosts, if they are there, are benevolent and only engage in pranks, like turning the jukebox, lights and water on and off at will. Matt believes that they know the owners and patrons mean them no harm and are happy to coexist but just can't

The Nick Fink building looks as if it has changed little since it was built in 1884. *Norma Lewis.*

Nick Fink's manager, Matt Rule, in front of a safe that was original to the building in 1924. *Norma Lewis.*

resist having a little fun. Resident ghosts are a good marketing tool, so every year on the three Sundays before Halloween, ghost hunters are invited to tour the upstairs, where the spirits reside.

There's a special each night, and all are excellent pub grub: Mile-High Nachos, Fink's Double Burger and a favorite, the Monster Burritos. The ghosts have yet to divulge their preferences.

The building retains its historic look, although it has undergone some renovations. Tin tiles are on the ceiling, and stained-glass shades adorn most of the overhead lights. A safe, made in Detroit in 1923, is original to the building. The bar and seemingly old-fashioned refrigerators keep the brews cold. A lone pool table invites competitions. Newer features are the outdoor dining patio and multiple large-screen televisions. Spend a few minutes with Matt Rule and two things become apparent: he loves Nick Fink's and he loves Nick Fink's history. Ghosts and all.

Over the years, other area buildings have allegedly been thought of as haunted as well. One of those was the Horseshoe Bar in the old Lamar Hotel. When the 333 Grandville Avenue, SW, building was remodeled, a secret room was discovered that is believed to have been used for hiding alcoholic beverages during Prohibition. Odd noises (including footsteps), handprints, unexplained scents and things generally going bump in the night added to the mystery. Presumably the spirits have been exorcised and identified as a man and a small child.

ROSE'S

Rose's, also a Gilmore holding, has a long East Grand Rapids history, starting with the fabled Ramona Park. The amusement park extraordinaire began in the 1890s with three pavilions on Reed's Lake. Whatever you might have wanted, this place had it. Along with local luminaries, nationally acclaimed stars performed. Among them were Jack Benny, Fanny Brice, Fred Allen, Will Rogers and Buster Keaton. Harry Houdini appeared there, and lecturers included Carrie Nation and Clarence Darrow.

There were the usual House of Mirrors and Laughing Gallery type of attractions. A popular roller coaster and Ferris wheel promised thrills, but the crowning jewels were the three carousel organs: the Sadie Mae, the Madam Laura and Big Bertha.

Dining and snacking options were everywhere, from full-scale service in the Chateau nightclub to hot dog and burger stands to an ice cream parlor located in the theater building. And then there was the venerable Rose's Popcorn. But popcorn wasn't all the Rose family offered park attendees. There was also Rose's Swimming School, and the popcorn shop grew into a short-order sandwich shop.

Today, Ramona Park is a distant memory. Rose's is the only physical reminder of the former glory on Reed's Lake. Sitting placidly on the lakeshore, with views from inside as well as outside on the deck, it is now an upscale dining spot. It almost didn't happen. The Rose family wanted to sell, but getting approval from the city proved difficult. Concern over ample parking, among other issues, nearly derailed the mission. Bob "Bub" Rose Jr. kept the sandwich shop open until the Gilmore Collection was finally able to buy the property and allay all the concerns.

The modern-day restaurant hasn't completely lost touch with its past. On the fireplace hangs a large copper kettle of popcorn above a plaque stating that it is "Bub's Last Batch." Instead of a mint or fortune cookie, diners are given a small paper cup of caramel corn at the end of their meal.

When it comes to ice cream parlors, folks usually gravitate to the one in the neighborhood. For those living in East Grand Rapids, a pleasant summer day used to mean lunch at Rose's, shopping at Jacobson's, strolling

Rose's is all that is left of the glorious Ramona Park, and the brass container of popcorn gives a nod to its first life as a popcorn shop. The plaque reads, "Bub's Last Batch" (referring to Bob Rose). *Norma Lewis.*

through the city's one-of-a-kind shops and then indulging in a waffle cone at the Jersey Junction. The Jersey Junction ice cream shop is owned by Doris "Chris" Van Allsburg, who is the mother of children's author and illustrator Chris Van Allsburg, winner of two Caldecott Medals. He is a Grand Rapids native and probably best known for the *Polar Express* and *Jumanji* books. Had Jacobson's Department Store not closed, that would still define a perfect day. There are, however, many other shops to investigate.

Rose's has long since outgrown its popcorn and snack shop beginning, but the large copper kettle mounted on the fireplace pays homage to its humble past.

THE COTTAGE BAR

Since 1927, the Cottage Bar in downtown GR has served up some of the best pub grub around, and it remains a popular gathering spot. Earl Coon opened it during Prohibition, so it wasn't called a bar until later. A card room and other enticements made it a fun place to be even in the absence of alcohol. Michigan was the first state to initiate prohibition and banned alcohol two years ahead of the rest of the country.

By 1933, the days of bathtub gin had drawn to a close, and saloon doors could swing open again. The Cottage was one of first local restaurants to be awarded a liquor license, and it is the oldest continuously operating bar and restaurant in the downtown area, where it remains an icon. Pete Vranos owned and operated the Cottage in the 1950s and sold it to John Verhill in 1967. He operated it until turning it over to his son, Dan, in 1980.

Dan and his wife, Lisa, now operate the restaurant and the adjoining One Trick Pony. They hadn't planned to run another restaurant, but they were forced to buy the building, as it was the only way they could buy the Cottage Bar space they were leasing. Over the years, the One Trick Pony site has been home to several businesses, including the West Michigan Tourist Association.

They are doing a fantastic job of operating both restaurants, as they do not compete with each other. The Pony has a more sophisticated menu and live music, while the Cottage Bar continues to be what it has always been. One innovation the Verhills have brought is outdoor seating, an idea Dan put into place after enjoying the patio of a California bar while on vacation.

Over the years, it caught on with various groups in the city, and that remains true today. It is a watering hole for the Heritage Hill neighborhood, and now the city has seen an influx of condominiums and loft housing. The Cottage has always been popular with choir members of nearby churches, who stop in after their weekly practices. The after-theater crowd finds it a pleasant spot for a nightcap. Students are drawn from Grand Rapids Community College and the Grand Valley State University downtown campus.

It is rumored that George C. Scott visited the Cottage while in town filming *Hardcore*, released in 1979, but Dan has not been able to verify that. The working title was *Pilgrim* during filming so as not to offend the Calvinistic sensibilities of some of the city residents. Grand Rapids–born Paul Schrader was the director, and George C. Scott's brother-in-law in the film was played by another area native, Dick Sargeant.

Dan can vouch for Michael Keaton and Howie Mandell, as he met both personally. There are no pictures to prove it because the Cottage Bar is a place where one's privacy is respected. Hollywood luminaries are not the only celebrities drawn to the Cottage when in the area. Former Detroit Tigers pitcher Dave Rozema, another local boy who made good, stopped at the Cottage during the spring of 2015 wearing his 1984 championship ring. He asked Dan if he remembered that was the last year the Tigers took the

The Cottage Bar is the oldest bar in continuous operation in the downtown area. *Grand Rapids Public Library.*

Members of the West Michigan Writers' Workshop get together to exchange ideas following the weekly critique meeting. *Shelby Ayers.*

World Series. "How could I forget?" Dan asked, like any other fan who starts each season with high hopes, only to see those hopes dashed. Again.

One first notices the relative quiet of the Cottage bar. Only one television is playing, and that is at the end of the bar. At the tables and booths, conversations can be had and ideas shared. It's that kind of place. A bulletin board proudly displays the covers of six books that were hatched when people got together there and talked.

From the dark wood paneling, booths and chairs to the cozy fireplace and abundance of decorative signs, it adds up to the ambience of a place where old friends gather and where new friends are quickly made.

MAGGIE'S KITCHEN

Magdalena (Maggie) Garcia was born in Chicago, but her family moved back to Mexico when she was three years old. She has been cooking since she was old enough to hold a spoon and stir and has worked in many restaurants, including the four-star French kitchen at the Chicago's Hyatt Regency Hotel. She remembered, and still practices, the best advice she received from her mother: "Everything fresh."

Her first visit to Grand Rapids convinced her that this is where she wanted to be. She cooked for Martin Morales in the Little Mexico Café and opened her own place, the award-winning Maggie's Kitchen, almost by accident. She and her late husband, Eustacio, owned and operated Moctezuma, a wholesale restaurant and grocery supply business to produce authentic Mexican seasonings among other products. Customers often came in while she was cooking lunch for her family and employees. The mouthwatering aroma of chiles, onions, chicken and beef made them want to buy her food.

The restaurant serves authentic Mexican food, including dishes difficult, if not impossible, to find north of the border. One of those authentic specialties is her customer-favorite soup called menudo. She serves it only on weekends because of the lengthy preparation. Menudo is made from the stomach lining of a cow, but before it can even be started, the meat has to soak in water overnight. After that, she cuts it into bite-sized pieces and boils it for three hours. Finally, it is time to make the soup. She adds the other ingredients and lets it simmer on the stovetop until it all blends into a rich and satisfying reminder of the homeland many of her regulars have left behind.

Fortunately for the rest of us, patrons can still experience those aromas, produced by Maggie herself. She still cooks every day, along with her employees and family members. Maggie's Kitchen's popularity was verified a few years ago when Konkle's, the bar next door, wanted to buy her building for expansion. Public outcry nipped that in the bud. Maggie Garcia still rules on Bridge Street.

Nothing here is made ahead and microwaved. Four generations of Maggie's family chop the fresh ingredients, stuff the taco shells, cook the enchiladas, heat beans, sprinkle cheese and plate the food. Food made from Maggie's own recipes helps to assure devotees that Maggie's Kitchen will be serving up those tasty nachos, Huevos à la Mexicana and Fajitas de Pollo for a long time to come.

All of this is enjoyed in a pleasant atmosphere. Plants thrive in the sunny storefront windows, and two of the flowerpots are adorned with American flags. Hungry folks line up to order and then watch the cooks prepare their feast. Mexican-themed posters adorn the wall, along with framed photos and awards Maggie has received.

One photograph is of Maggie with Grand Rapids mayor George Heartwell. The mayor is holding his restaurant favorite, Maggie's Chicken Platter.

ARNIE'S BAKERY AND RESTAURANTS

The large number of Dutch immigrants would seem to indicate an abundance of Dutch eateries, but this it not really true. The frugal immigrants ate at home for the most part, and not just to save money but because the home-cooking tasted better. Restaurants came, but that was much later.

The Arnie's Bakery and Restaurant local chain celebrated its centennial in 2005, although it has experienced several names and personas over the years. Three Dutch brothers—Arnold, John and Chris Sonneveldt—founded the company in 1905 and named it the Crescent Bakery. Arnold Sonneveldt Jr. renamed it Sonneveldt. In the early 1930s, the family changed the name again, this time to Butternut Bakery. Arnold Sr. worked as a baker in the Netherlands before immigrating to the United States.

Then a Swede, Arne Fahlen, became a partner. In 1972, Fahlen decided it was time to branch out. He opened the first of the company's restaurants in suburban Rockford, although he named it the Old Mill in Rockford because it was housed in a historic old mill. One of the Old Mill's specialties was legendary sandwiches with meats and cheeses piled high on thick-

The Old Mill Bakery and Restaurant in suburban Rockford was later acquired by Arnie's Bakery and Restaurant. The old part shown here is used for private parties. *Norma Lewis.*

sliced bread from the company bakery. Bakery-fresh desserts kept patrons returning for more.

It took until 1978 for the Arnie's name to appear on the new Leonard Street restaurant location and on the bakery products as well. The names Arnold and Arne made the name a no-brainer, and the chain grew to five restaurants, with bakery products now found in local supermarkets and other outlets.

Fahlen bought the company from the Sonneveldts in 1992. Arnie's is still a family enterprise, as Arne's sons—Rich, Jim and Erik—run the business with their dad. Both the Sonneveldts and the Fahlens have always supported the local community, giving generously to Meijer Gardens, the Mel Trotter Mission and many more.

Russ'

The first restaurant of the local chain Russ' opened in 1934 in nearby Holland, advertising Russ' All Steak Hamburgs. The owner, Russell Bouws, came from a German immigrant family from a village just outside the Netherlands at a time when the borders were indistinct. Like other families in that location, they were bound by religion and thought themselves more Dutch than Deutsch. Russ' was a huge success, serving up burgers and fries, but it was the homemade pies that put it on the map—Dutch apple, strawberry, blueberry, custard and more.

Over the years, the company expanded, opening its first Grand Rapids restaurant on Twenty-eighth Street near the malls. No curb service here, only the same good food at reasonable prices. Two favorite items were a tuna salad and fried chicken. And let's not forget the pies—lemon meringue, chocolate, banana cream and others.

The second Grand Rapids Russ' came soon after, also on Twenty-eighth Street but at the other end in Wyoming. Today, there are twelve, half of which are in the Grand Rapids area and the rest not far away. Décor is Dutch and varies, but framed historic images of the company, windmills and tulips are common themes. The restaurants all remain true to their conservative Dutch roots, and none is open on Sundays. So far, that hasn't caused them to lose business the rest of the week, as they serve a clientele that shares the same values.

THE CHOO CHOO

Not everyone chooses to get their burgers at fast-food chains. Anyone who has ever had one would rather have those at the Choo Choo, an iconic red landmark on the northeast corner of Plainfield Avenue and Leonard Street. Long before the building was painted caboose red, it served as a Shipman Coal Company office. In its new life, it has been grilling what the Coke sign says are "the best hamburgers on earth—or anywhere else" since 1940, when the burgers were five for one dollar. It has remained in the same family since 1957, as current owner, Rick Mack, acquired the business from his father-in-law. One of the house specialties is the Red Caboose Deluxe Cheeseburger, a half-pound patty served on a grilled bun with choice of toppings. Those who are really hungry can opt for the Legend Deluxe and feast on a whole-pound burger. If you're really, really hungry, order it with steak fries and a peanut butter malt. Diners can choose from a full range of burgers, other sandwiches and salads, along with a full breakfast menu. The burgers are the most popular, and the friendly staff serves up about five hundred per week.

The Choo Choo is also known for its shakes and malts, with the peanut butter shake being the most popular. No need for appetizers here, as the grill is in the corner of the dining area. If the mouthwatering aromas fail to whet your appetite, nothing will.

The staff at the space-challenged Choo Choo restaurant: owner Rick Mack with Kathy Spencer (left) and Annette Ries. *Shelby Ayers.*

Once an office of the Shipman Coal Company, this cozy building has been home to the Choo Choo since 1940. *Shelby Ayers.*

It's a fun place. People don't take themselves too seriously here. As the name hints, the décor is trains, trains and more trains. Some were found at garage sales, and others were gifts from patrons. One is an original drawing, produced by a regular sitting on the curb across the street with his sketch pad. The rail theme was a natural, as the location was beside tracks. The color suggests a caboose.

So does the size. This space-challenged eatery contains two booths and ten counter stools, and those stools are so close together you can't help rubbing elbows with those seated beside you. You will likely also rub shoulders, knees and arms and maybe even play footsie. That closeness contributes to a cozy ambience that makes it hard not to get caught up in conversations. Some of the clientele has been coming here for years, the result being friendly banter between the servers and the served. It may be the only restaurant where you will hear a regular explaining why he or she won't be in for lunch on the following day. Excuses are not required, but folks might worry if you failed to show up.

On a dreary June Monday, the day after Father's Day, lunch regulars have filled every available seat, while others stand in line waiting for takeout orders. Conversations revolve around how the holiday was spent. To find the restroom, one must go into the kitchen and hang a left at the fridge. A sign informs one and all that the North Pole is 6,843 miles away. This is Michigan, however, so there are times when that distant landmark feels much closer.

Rick has no need to advertise, as the place is usually filled to capacity. Social media spreads the word, and before that, popularity grew by word of mouth. Anyone who wants him to expand should consider the wisdom of the old saying, "If it ain't broke, don't fix it." The Choo Choo ain't broke and doesn't need to be fixed.

YESTERDOG

A fun spot for those preferring hot dogs has long been Yesterdog in the trendy East Town neighborhood. Yesterdog started as a hole in the wall at its Wealthy Street location and became so popular that it has expanded over the years until now there is a back entrance on Lake Street.

Dogs are served here—all manner of dogs. Chili dogs, kraut dogs, vegetarian dogs and Yesterdogs. The vegetarian option is not a sausage made of soybeans or other veggie products; rather, it is a dogless bun stuffed with all the usual toppings. Diners order their dog of choice, usually more than one, along with a Pepsi and bag of chips.

Snapshots of patrons past and present cover the lower portion of the walls and are a testament to a rabid fan base. Some show people wearing Yesterdog T-shirts and caps in the far corners of the world. One is a bridal couple in full wedding regalia eating a Yesterdog from opposite ends. The person who delivered the dog is visible and sporting the company shirt and cap. You will also find snaps of local and state celebrities, including former U.S. senator Carl Levin and former governor Jennifer Granholm.

The restaurant itself is treasure-trove of memorabilia. Despite serving only Pepsi products, décor includes an oversized Coke dispenser, and one of the many signs on the walls is a street sign reading, "R.C. Cola Lane." A piano sits at the ready along with pedal cars, and a large wooden model airplane is suspended from the tin ceiling. Initials carved on the high-backed booths made of dark wood provide a roster of who loved whom over the decades, along with a smattering of telephone numbers.

Marge's Donut Den

Just when you think Marge Wilson, owner of Marge's Donut Den, has done everything possible to offer her patrons the kind of personal experiences not found in Krispy Kreme or Dunkin' Donuts, she ups the ante by hosting a weekend-long fortieth anniversary celebration (in June 2015). The weekend events included something for everyone. Saturday's lineup started with a Catholic Mass. Then came Freddie the Clown, Kids Donut Decorating, music by the Silvertones and a Grand Rapids accordion concert. Sunday, which was also Father's Day, had a Protestant church service, lunch and concerts. And that doesn't count the donuts and other baked goods, all sold at 1975 prices.

Since opening her popular shop, Marge has been the poster child for community involvement. To that end, she has allowed her building to be used for Bible study groups and Lego events, and she even held a wedding there for a couple unable to pay for a dream wedding but yearning for something more meaningful than a quick stop at city hall. A South High School alumni group meets there regularly. The piano in the corner hints that people do more here than eat donuts.

As far as the donuts go, they have been voted Michigan's best in the MLive poll. With upward of sixty bakery products from which to choose, it would impossible not to find something tempting—usually a great many somethings, like the long johns, the apple fritters and the glazed, sugared, chocolated and more. It isn't all about donuts, either. Need a decorated special occasion cake, cupcakes, cookies with frosting, cookies with sprinkles, maple frosted bars, pumpkin bars or almost anything else you can imagine? This is your go-to place.

Marge is known for her generosity in donating donuts to worthy causes and also for her creativity in coming up with new product ideas, like guitar-shaped donuts for Brad Paisley and his entourage during a Grand Rapids appearance. They proved so popular that she still offers guitar-shaped cookies. One of the major reasons businesses go stale is because the owners turn off their creativity. That will never happen here because this owner never stops dreaming up new products or new ways to make her community a better place.

She opens her shop on Christmas to serve those patrons who have nowhere else to go. It's possible that some of them really do have other places to go but just prefer being with her. The saying painted on the outside of the building, "Where old friends meet and make new friends," isn't empty talk. Like Marge herself, it's the real thing.

The shop is inviting. While many customers stop and grab a dozen donuts to take to wherever they are going, just as many choose to come in and sit a spell. They know people here and look forward to seeing friends. Marge knows that and reserves a large round table covered with a white tablecloth for her regulars. They range from young to a feisty octogenarian who answers to the nickname "Trouble." Drop in sometime and maybe she will tell you why.

BYRON CENTER

Suburban Byron Center is home to the old Byron Center Hotel, now simply called the Byron, and owned since 2009 by Dennis Klinge. The hotel site was first owned by William and Ellie Baker. Their son, Charlie, and daughter-in-law, Rosalie, rebuilt and opened the hotel in 1902 after it had been destroyed by fire three years earlier. In 1903, it was open for business and had a saloon on the west side, but no women were allowed inside.

Back in its heyday, folks drove from as far away as Muskegon to line up outside for the signature Saturday night fried chicken dinners. Today, the famous chicken is on the menu almost every day, and what were once hotel rooms are now rented by the month.

Above: Wedding portrait of Charlie and Rose Baker of Byron Center. After their marriage, Charlie ran the Byron Hotel owned by Rose's father. *Byron Center Museum*.

Opposite: The Byron Hotel would become famous in later years for its fried chicken dinners, originally served only on Saturday nights. *Byron Center Museum*.

The Byron Hotel has long been famous throughout the area for all its chickens—the ones it fries up golden brown and the iconic twelve-foot concrete chicken now adorning the parking lot but once in front of the building. It was stolen in 2009 in what might have been a prank, as it would be difficult to hide a concrete chunk of that size for very long. Not to worry, though; the purloined poultry has been restored to its rightful place and once again provides a photo op for patrons and passerby.

The only problem with the hotel is that Byron Center is an ultraconservative community, and a line that can't be crossed exists between those who do and those who do not (consume alcohol, that is). There are those who refuse to darken its door. For them, the first choice of local dining is the Byron Family Restaurant, a longtime favorite with the local Dutch community. The restaurant opened in the 1950s and has been in the Palmbos family since 1978, when Jack Palmbos assumed ownership. Jack's son, Matt, has owned it since 2003.

The food is simple, good and affordably priced, exactly what Matt's guests are looking for. His crowd-pleasing Thursday night buffet includes chicken wings, smoked sausage and meatballs, along with sides, a generous salad bar and desserts. It's the kind of place where people pray before eating and play what insiders call Dutch Bingo. In the close-knit Dutch culture, if you talk to someone long enough you are likely to find out you are distantly related. Bingo! Matt can't claim a chicken statue, but until recently, he had another monument just outside his door: a veterans memorial in the shape of a huge rock. It has since been moved to a new location in front of the township building.

In either of the Byron Center restaurants, you will be noticed when you come in for the first time. The local folks are friendly but curious. They want to know who you are and, even more important, who your grandfather was. If they ask if you are from "up north," they don't mean the Upper Peninsula; they mean McBain and the surrounding area. Many of them came from there, and you might be a long-lost cousin several times removed. Bingo!

Recipes

CHURCHILL'S OYSTERS ROCKEFELLER
(AMWAY GRAND PLAZA HOTEL)

6 fresh oysters in half shell
8 ounces fish stock (or slightly salted water)
8 ounces fresh spinach, chopped
1 ounce onions, finely chopped
2 ounces cream
1 ounce Purnel liqueur
bread crumbs

Crack open oysters. Remove from shell and simmer in stock for about 2 minutes. Put back in shells.

ROCKEFELLER MIX
Sauté spinach and onions until onions are clear. Add cream and Purnel. Simmer 5 minutes. Add bread crumbs to thicken. Pour mixture over oysters. Transfer oysters to ovenproof platter. Bake at 350° Fahrenheit for 5 to 7 minutes until heated. Makes 1 serving.

CHURCHILL'S VEAL FINANCIER

8 ounces veal filets
1 ounce clarified butter
1 large mushroom, sliced
1 ounce cooking sherry
2 ounces beef stock

Sauté veal in butter until lightly browned on both sides. Add mushroom and gently stir. Add sherry and beef stock. Cook over low heat until sauce is reduced to a fine glaze. Place veal on plate and top with sauce. Makes 1 serving.

DUCKLING À LA MONROE CAFÉ (PANTLIND HOTEL)

1 5-pound duckling
2 medium oranges
1 lemon
½ cup sugar
1 teaspoon currant jelly
1 quart brown sauce
1 teaspoon cornstarch
½ cup dry sherry
watercress

Preheat oven to 350° Fahrenheit. Place duck in roasting pan. Prick skin of duck and roast for 2 hours. Peel outer skin from the oranges and lemon. Cut skin into fine strips. Heat sugar in heavy saucepan until it is caramelized deep brown. Add currant jelly and juice from the oranges and lemon.

Remove duck from pan. Keep warm. Pour off fat. Add a little hot water and scrape off all duck juices from bottom of pan. Pour into large saucepan with brown sauce. Add caramelized sugar and orange and lemon strips. Stir thoroughly. Dilute cornstarch with sherry and add to sauce. Simmer for 20 minutes.

Halve the duck. Remove breast bones and reheat whole duck in oven for a few minutes. Pour sauce over duck. Garnish each serving with sliced oranges and watercress. Makes 2 servings.

SCHNITZELBANK'S SAUERBRATEN

½ cup dry red wine
2 cups cold water
8 peppercorns
½ cup red wine vinegar
1 medium onion, sliced
3 bay leaves
4 pounds bottom beef roast, trimmed
3 tablespoons lard or vegetable oil
½ cup onions, chopped
½ cup carrots, chopped
¼ cup celery, chopped
2 tablespoons flour
2 cups reserved marinade
½ cup water
½ cup gingersnap cookies, crumbled

In 3-quart saucepan, combine dry red wine, cold water, peppercorns, red wine vinegar, onion and bay leaves. Bring to a boil; remove from heat and cool to room temperature. Place beef in deep crock or nonreactive container and pour marinade over meat. Liquid should come halfway up sides of roast. Cover and refrigerate for 3 days, turning roast each day. Remove roast from marinade; pat dry with paper towels. Strain marinade and retain liquid. Discard spices and sliced onion.

In a 5-quart roasting pan, warm lard or oil over high heat. Add the meat and brown on all sides. Transfer meat to platter. Save 2 tablespoons of pan drippings in roasting pan. Add chopped onions, carrots and celery to drippings. Cook 5 minutes over medium heat, until vegetables are light brown. Add flour and cook 5 minutes longer. Add 2 cups reserved marinade and ½ cup water. Bring to a boil.

Place roast back in pan and cover. Bake at 350° Fahrenheit for 2 hours.

Remove roast to platter and cover with foil to retain heat. Pour liquid from roasting pan into a saucepan and skim off surface fat. Add ½ cups crumbled gingersnap cookies and cook 10 minutes, stirring often. Strain and return liquid to saucepan. Let simmer until ready to serve.

Slice roast into medium-thick slices and arrange on platter. Serve with the sauce and boiled potatoes, dumplings, noodles and red cabbage on the side. Makes 6–8 servings.

SCHNITZELBANK'S POTATO PANCAKES

8 medium russet potatoes (about 2½ pounds)
1 large onion
2 eggs, separated
2 tablespoons flour
1 scant tablespoon salt
1 teaspoon white pepper
canola oil

Peel potatoes and cover with cold water until ready to make pancakes. Grate potatoes and onion, alternately, into a strainer set over a bowl to catch juices. Onion juice will help prevent potatoes from darkening. Using wooden spoon or hands, press or squeeze out as much liquid as possible. Reserve all liquid and let it settle in a bowl for 2 to 3 minutes.

Combine pressed potato and onion in another bowl. Carefully pour off watery part of reserved liquid, but do not discard thick starchy paste at bottom of bowl. Scrape up starchy paste and add to potato mixture.

Add egg yolks, flour, salt and pepper; mix thoroughly. In separate bowl, beat egg whites with electric mixer until stiff and shiny peaks form. Fold into potato mixture.

Preheat oven to 250° Fahrenheit. Set rack on baking sheet or shallow pan.

In heavy cast-iron skillet, heat ½ inch of canola oil. Using about 2 tablespoons batter per pancake, drop into hot oil and fry, turning once, until deep golden brown on both sides, about 10 minutes for each batch. Make sure to fry them one at a time to allow oil to reheat before adding another. Drain on paper towels and then transfer to rack and keep warm in oven while frying remaining pancakes.

Do not hold pancakes for more than 15 minutes before serving or they may become soggy. Serve with homemade applesauce or sour cream. Makes 6 servings.

LES IDEES' SHRIMP CHARTREUSE
(VARIATION OF SHRIMP DE JONGHE)

12 medium shrimp
⅛ cup scallions, chopped
¼ teaspoon garlic powder
⅛ teaspoon white pepper
¼ teaspoon seasoning salt
2 tablespoons butter, melted
3 ounces bread crumbs
1 ounce Chartreuse

Shell, devein and butterfly shrimp and then place in a round baking dish. Sauté scallions, garlic powder, white pepper and seasoning salt in half the melted butter until clear. Add bread crumbs and mix to moisten. Sprinkle crumb mixture over shrimp. Pour remaining melted butter on top. Bake at 350° Fahrenheit for 7 minutes. Flame with Chartreuse. The Chartreuse will extinguish on its own. Makes 1 serving.

THREE CROWN'S HAMBURGER PIE

1½ pound ground round
½ cup cracker crumbs
2 eggs
½ cup milk
½ cup onion, chopped
1 teaspoon salt
½ teaspoon pepper
4 slices processed cheese
2 cups mashed potatoes
1 can mushroom soup
¼ cup milk

Preheat oven to 350° Fahrenheit. Mix ground beef, cracker crumbs, eggs, milk, onion, salt and pepper together in a bowl. Put in 9-inch pie plate. Bake at 350° for 30 minutes. Drain grease. Top with cheese slices. Cover with mashed potatoes. Mix half of soup with ¼ cup milk and spread over top of pie. Bake until light brown, about 15 minutes.

SAYFEE'S EAST STEAK DIANE

2 tablespoons butter
¼ cup scallions, chopped
½ cup fresh mushrooms, sliced
1 clove garlic, chopped
¼ cup Burgundy wine
⅛ cup half and half
10 ounces strip steak
1 teaspoon brandy

Melt butter in skillet. Add scallions, mushrooms and garlic. Sauté 2 minutes over medium heat. Add wine and cream, stirring gently until combined. Add steak. Sauté 2 to 3 minutes on each side. Add brandy. Flame. Makes 1 serving.

SAYFEE'S EAST AMBROSIA (VEAL AND SCAMPI)

5 ounces scampi
1 4-ounce veal steak or scallop
¼ cup au jus
1 tablespoon sherry
1 tablespoon sauterne wine
1 clove garlic, chopped
¼ cup scallions, chopped
1 tablespoon brandy

Shell and devein scampi; remove tails. Flatten veal until approximately ¾-inch thick. Pour au jus, sherry and sauterne into large skillet. Add veal and scampi, garlic and scallions. Sauté 4 minutes, turning veal once. Add brandy. Flame. Serve immediately with remaining sauce poured over meat. Makes 1 serving.

BAVARIAN HAUS BRAISED STUFFED BEEF ROLLS

8 thin slices top beef round
1 medium onion, chopped
¼ pound bacon, diced
¼ cup flour
1 teaspoon paprika
2 tablespoons cooking oil
1 small onion or leek, sliced
¼ cup coarsely cut parsley
1 cup hot water
1 tablespoon cornstarch
2 tablespoons cold water

Pound beef slices with mallet until very thin. Divide onion and bacon among the beef slices, placing them across one end. Roll up with filling in center; secure rolls with toothpicks. Sprinkle all sides of rolls with flour, paprika, salt and pepper. In a large skillet, brown in oil on all sides. Add onion or leek and parsley. Add hot water. Cover and simmer until tender, about 1½ to 2 hours. Remove rolls, carefully remove toothpicks and keep rolls warm. Strain and measure 1 cup liquid from skillet. Stir cornstarch into cold water and add to measured meat juices. Cook over medium heat, stirring constantly, until thickened. Serve the gravy with the rolls. Makes 4 servings.

LES IDEES ST. ELMO'S OMELET

1 ounce butter
3 eggs
3 ounces lump crabmeat
2 ounces Mornay sauce
2 slices toast

Place butter in nonstick omelet pan and heat over high flame. Beat eggs until yolks and whites are combined. Pour into pan and, as eggs set, tilt the pan so that raw egg mixture slides under and sets. Alternate tilting with gentle stirring. Once eggs have set, flip and cook briefly until slightly golden. Stir in crab. Fold onto plate. Top with Mornay Sauce and serve with buttered toast. Makes 1 serving.

SUN SAI GAI'S DRAGON AND PHOENIX (SHRIMP AND CHICKEN STIR-FRIED WITH ASSORTED VEGETABLES)

Stir-fry 1 pound medium shrimp, peeled and deveined, and 5 pieces of chicken.

STIR IN:
15 ounces can baby corn
black mushrooms
sliced carrots
sliced water chestnuts
broccoli
Chinese cabbage
1 cup chicken broth

Vary amount of vegetables according to taste and size of crowd.

GRAVY
1 teaspoon oyster sauce
1 teaspoon monosodium glutamate
$\frac{1}{2}$ teaspoon cornstarch
1 teaspoon sherry wine
1 teaspoon soy sauce
$\frac{1}{2}$ teaspoon salt
$\frac{1}{2}$ teaspoon sesame oil

Pour vegetables into the gravy and stir-fry together about 5 minutes. Makes 5 servings.

TOOTSIE VAN KELLY'S MICHIGAN SWEET CHILI

2 pounds ground beef
2 cups stewed tomatoes
2 cups Mexican red chili beans
1 cup tomato juice
5 tablespoons sugar
$\frac{1}{4}$ cup chili powder (start with less and adjust to taste)

Brown ground beef and pour off fat. Mix in all other ingredients. Simmer on low heat, approximately 1 hour.

ARNIE'S BAKERY AND RESTAURANT VIKING SANDWICH

1 whole grain sandwich roll
mayonnaise
Havarti cheese
1 broiled sirloin patty
1 smoked ham slice
tomato slices
lettuce

Split roll and toast. Spread mayonnaise. Add cheese. Place sirloin patty, ham slice, tomato and lettuce on bottom half of roll. Add top half. Makes 1 sandwich.

ARNIE'S BAKERY AND RESTAURANT SCANDINAVIAN SHUFFLE

pita bread
sliced roast beef or smoked ham
Danish cheese
tomato slices
lettuce
sour cream
red onion slice, chopped (optional)

Grill pita bread. Wrap around meat, cheese, tomatoes, lettuce, sour cream, and onions. Serve with cucumber salad. Makes 1 sandwich.

KUM BAK RELISH

1 small bunch celery, finely diced
1 large onion, finely diced
1 10-ounce jar sweet pickle relish
1 small bottle ketchup
¼ cup mustard
¼ cup vinegar
2 tablespoons sugar

In large saucepan, combine celery, onion, relish, ketchup, mustard, vinegar and sugar. Bring to a boil. Process in hot water bath for 5 minutes. Spoon into clean pint jars. Makes 2 pints. Nutrition information per 1 tablespoon serving: 17 calories, 0 protein, 0 fat, 4 grams carbohydrate, 0 fiber, 0 cholesterol and 133 milligrams sodium.

Mr. Steak's Dapper Apple

BATTER
1 cup Drake's Batter Mix
1 tablespoon cinnamon
1 tablespoon sugar
1 cup water

PRALINE SAUCE
4 ounces butter (do not use margarine)
2 tablespoons water
$\frac{1}{2}$ cup brown sugar, firmly packed
$\frac{1}{4}$ cup chopped pecans

4 medium apples
cooking oil
vanilla ice cream

BATTER
With wire whisk, combine batter mix, cinnamon and sugar. Add water. Whisk until smooth. Set aside.

SAUCE
Melt butter. Add water and brown sugar. Stir over low heat until thick and smooth. Add pecans and keep warm.

APPLES
Peel, core and cut apples into wedges. Put wedges on bamboo or metal skewers. Dip in batter and deep-fry in 3 inches of cooking oil heated to 350° Fahrenheit for 3 minutes. Top each serving with a scoop of vanilla ice cream. Pour warm sauce over apples and ice cream. Makes 4 servings.

BILL KNAPP'S CHOCOLATE CAKE AND ICE CREAM DESSERT CAKE

CAKE
1 10-ounce box devil's food cake mix
1½ cups warm water
2 large eggs

TOPPING
½ cup butter (do not substitute margarine)
12 ounces semisweet chocolate chips
1 14-ounce can sweetened condensed milk
14 ounces light Karo syrup

vanilla ice cream

CAKE
Preheat oven to 325° Fahrenheit. Using an electric mixer set on medium, beat together cake mix, water and eggs until smooth. Pour into greased and floured 9x13 cake pan. Bake 30 to 35 minutes or until cake tester inserted in center comes out clean.

TOPPING
Simmer water in bottom of double boiler. In top, combine butter, chocolate chips, condensed milk and Karo syrup

Cut cake into squares. Pour topping over squares. Add 1 scoop of vanilla ice cream and serve.

THREE CROWNS APPLE BAR

CRUST
1⅛ cups shortening
3 cups flour
3 eggs
water

FILLING
4 cups tart apples, peeled and sliced
1 teaspoon cinnamon
⅞ cup granulated sugar
2 tablespoons flour

GLAZE
1 cup powdered sugar
2 tablespoons milk

CRUST
Preheat oven to 350° Fahrenheit. Cut shortening into flour. Put eggs into a cup, beat together and then add enough water to fill the cup. Add to flour and shortening mixture; mix well. Divide dough in half. Roll each half to fit cookie sheet.

FILLING
Mix apples, cinnamon, sugar, and flour. Spread on bottom crust. Add top crust and bake for 30 to 35 minutes at 350°. Drizzle glaze over top while still hot.

GLAZE
Combine ingredients in small saucepan, stir over low heat until glazed. If too thick, add a few drops of water.

TOOTSIE VAN KELLY'S WATERMELON SHOOTER

⅓ ounce vodka
⅓ ounce strawberry liqueur
¼ ounce orange juice
¼ ounce lime juice

Shake ingredients together and pour over crushed ice. Makes 1 shooter.

Bibliography

Books

Belknap, Charles. *Yesterdays of Grand Rapids.* Grand Rapids, MI, n.d.

Gillis, Edward V. *Growing Up in Old Lithuanian Town.* Grand Rapids, MI: Grand Rapids Historical Commission, 2000.

Lydens, Z.Z. *A Look at Early Grand Rapids.* Grand Rapids, MI: Zondervan, 1981.

Snow, Gail Marie. *Remembering Ramona Park: A Passionate History of a Much Beloved Place.* Grand Rapids, MI: self-published, 2013.

Various Library Resources

Advance newspapers.

Grand Rapids and Grand Rapids suburban city directories.

Grand Rapids magazine.

Grand Rapids Press.

Grand Rapids telephone directories.

Grand Times.

Grand Valley History magazine.

Vertical files at the Grand Rapids Public Library.

INTERVIEWS

Dowdy, Matt. Gilmore Collection interview, May 19, 2015.

Forist, Alex. Grand Rapids Public Museum, June 29, 2015.

Klinge, Dennis. Byron Center Hotel, May 23, 2015.

Lobell, Jeff, owner of Beltline Bar and twelve other restaurants. June 15, 2015.

Palmbos, Matthew. Byron Family Restaurant, August 30, 2015

Snyder, Elaine. Byron Center Museum, Historical Society, June 3, 2015.

Verhill, Dan. Cottage Bar interview, June 14, 2015.

Index

About the Author

Norma Lewis has lived in or near the Grand Rapids area for more than twenty-five years. She is a member of the Grand Rapids Historical Society, the Grand Rapids Women's History Council and the Tri-Cities Historical Museum in Grand Haven. *Lost Restaurants of Grand Rapids* is Norma's ninth book. She has authored five books with Arcadia Publishing, three of them with her late husband, Jay de Vries, and has also published a children's book on the Transcontinental Railroad.